ETHNIC ST. LOUIS

Elizabeth Terry   John Wright   Patrick McCarthy

Press

Reedy Press
PO Box 5131
St. Louis, MO 63139, USA
www.reedypress.com

Library of Congress Control Number: 2015930930

ISBN: 9781935806998

Cover Design: Kevin Belford

Interior Design: Jill Halpin

Printed in the United States of America

15 16 17 18 19   5 4 3 2 1

TABLE OF CONTENTS

Asia

Hispanic Communities **137**

INTRODUCTION

St. Louis has long and deservedly enjoyed a reputation as one of America's oldest and finest cities. Its immigrant roots are deep. Yet the picture of immigration in St. Louis has dramatically changed in the last two centuries. To appreciate today's ethnic St. Louis and anticipate the future, one must understand the region's immigrant past.

Founded originally as a fur trading post in 1764, the city flourished at the confluence of the Mississippi and Missouri Rivers. These were the two dominant inland transportation routes to points west for much of the nineteenth century. Wave after wave of immigrants flocked to St. Louis on steamboats paddling upriver from New Orleans. Longtime Native American cultures gave way to the newer customs and beliefs of English, German, Irish, and other immigrants.

Many Germans settled on the west side of the Mississippi to work as merchants, frequently outfitting wagons for pioneers heading west. On the east side, others farmed pockets of land left by the English and other earlier immigrants. As the influx of Germans continued, communities like Belleville, Illinois, were formed.

By 1850, St. Louis was the eighth-largest city in the United States, and 50 percent of its residents were immigrants, mostly Germans and Irish. The city boasted a rich tapestry of cultures represented by reading rooms and saloons! Examples included Joseph Pulitzer, who, as a thirty-one-year-old Hungarian newcomer in 1878, founded the *St. Louis Post-Dispatch* newspaper. It was the beginning of his eventual publishing empire. Earlier, in 1852, Eberhard Anheuser had bought part ownership in the Bavarian Brewery, which would eventually become Anheuser-Busch. The Irish, on the other hand, were frequently uneducated with few skills. So they clustered in lower-level working-class jobs, sometimes in competition with freed African Americans.

By 1900, St. Louis had become the fourth-largest city in the United States. The 1904 World's Fair debuted on nearly thirteen hundred acres of land in Forest Park where the city also hosted the 1904 Summer Olympics. In all, an estimated twenty million visitors[1] attended. What a glowing tribute to St. Louis!

Unknown at the time, St. Louis's ranking among U.S. cities had peaked. By 1930, it had dropped to seventh and by 2012 to nineteenth. What happened?

One can argue that the seeds of St. Louis's decline were already sown by 1900. Dramatic changes had been taking place in the previous fifty years. And they cast an unfortunate shadow on St. Louis's continued rapid growth and competitive ranking.

Most consequential was the revolution in the mode of American inland transportation, which resulted in the rapid decline of steamboat traffic beginning in the mid-nineteenth century. At that time, St. Louis was the largest American city west of Pittsburgh and the second-largest port in the country. There was a drastic shift in the decades following the Civil War.

The evolution in transportation modes occurred in stages. Projects included the completion of the Erie Canal in 1825, which connected the Hudson River with Lake Erie, and the Illinois and Michigan Canal in 1848, which accomplished the same for the Upper Mississippi River and Lake Michigan. As a result, goods and passengers had more convenient access to the Great Lakes, Ohio, and Upper Mississippi River regions; long and expensive trips around the Florida peninsula and via New Orleans could now be avoided.

However, it was the completion of the one-thousand-eight-hundred-mile transcontinental railroad system in 1869 that dealt St. Louis its most severe blow. For the first time, the Atlantic and Pacific coasts were connected by rail, enabling goods and passengers to be transported faster and more affordably. And Chicago—not St. Louis—became the Midwest hub for the railroad system.

St. Louis continued to grow after 1850 but at a slower pace. Meanwhile, Chicago, which first appeared in the rankings in 1860 in ninth position, rose rapidly to second by 1900, where it remained until 2000 when it was replaced by Los Angeles.

Another change was masked in census figures for late nineteenth- and early twentieth-century St. Louis that demonstrated a dramatic decline in percent of immigrant residents. From a high of 50 percent foreign-born residents in 1850, St. Louis had dropped to 4.3 percent in 2012, with the bulk of the decline occurring before 1930. In fact, while St. Louis's ranking among cities was growing, the city's percent of immigrant representation dropped by more than 30 percent in the fifty years between 1850 and 1900.

The explanation for the decline again harks back to America's transportation revolution. St. Louis was not a port of entry for large numbers of newly arrived immigrants. Instead, immigrants arrived at coastal ports and frequently settled nearby. If they moved inland in the latter half of the nineteenth century, immigrants, like others, relied on railway transportation. Naturally, Chicago attracted the bulk of settlers because of its central and highly accessible location.

After 1924, nativism resulted in a variety of exclusionary laws limiting immigration for the next forty years. Few immigrants came to America in these years; those who did rarely ventured beyond the large coastal ports where they found language and cultural enclaves to ease their adjustment.

Meanwhile, St. Louis's population was rapidly growing as a result of internal migration, largely African Americans moving from the South in the first half of the twentieth century. The Great Migration resulted in massive cultural shifts in St. Louis, where now-famous musicians, including Scott Joplin, introduced ragtime and jazz and otherwise participated in the burgeoning music scene.

Today, St. Louis is much changed from its earliest roots, yet in other ways it remains the same. Residents revere their past and frequently visit the grounds of the former 1904 World's Fair, now the site of the world-renowned Saint Louis Zoo and Saint Louis Art Museum. The Grammy Award–winning St. Louis Symphony is among the best in America, as is the Cardinals baseball team, perennial playoff contenders.

The city's early immigrants—German, Irish, Italian, eastern European, and more—have been joined by more recent arrivals from all parts of the globe. They hail from

Africa, Asia, and Latin America in addition to the earlier European favorites. The variety is immense, but, as in the last century, our percent of immigrant residents has remained lower than the national average. It is, in fact, the lowest of the top twenty U.S. metropolitan areas.

In the past fifty years, the immigrants the city can claim have generally arrived by one of two routes. The first is as a foreign student at one of St. Louis's renowned universities. From there they have moved to local corporations and hospitals where they have helped create commerce and improve St. Louis's economy. Over the years, many of these university graduates have sponsored a variety of relatives who have helped build many St. Louis immigrant communities, including the Chinese, Indian, Filipino, and Korean groups.

The second route for St. Louis's immigrants is as refugees, escaping persecution in war-ravaged countries around the world. Private and faith-based organizations have assisted tens of thousands of refugees to resettle, including Bosnians who, with their American-born children, now number as many as fifty thousand. Most recently, they have been joined by Somalis and Bhutanese and by Iraqis and Afghans who worked with U.S. forces in those countries.

In both cases, immigration to St. Louis has been low profile and comparatively small, mirroring the immigrant experience of the past 150 years. As a result, St. Louis has suffered from severe population loss since the mid-twentieth century. City officials were surprised to learn after the 2010 census that the city's population had dropped to 319,000. It was at its smallest size in a century and reflected an 8 percent loss in a decade.[2] The St. Louis County population also dropped, albeit by only 1.7 percent, to fewer than one million people.[3]

There is optimism, however, that St. Louis's immigrant population will grow again. In 2012, a groundbreaking study[4] by economist Jack Strauss, then a professor at Saint Louis University, found that immigrants are an important source of entrepreneurship and new population, both essential to St. Louis's economic well-being. As a result, the St. Louis Mosaic Project, a combined city and county, public and private initiative, was founded to identify ways to attract and retain more immigrants. To do so, it is essential that St. Louis promote its values, provide key integrative services, and and most importantly create a welcoming environment for all—including new immigrants and those already residing in the region.

So, we are coming full circle. For St. Louis to be a successful and highly regarded city of the future, it must study its past, identify its strengths and weaknesses, and set forth a strong and positive road map. A key element of that plan must be understanding and appreciating the many aspects of culture and ethnicity on which St. Louis was founded. There is strength in diversity as long as residents are aware and appreciate the many differences of *all* its residents. Together, diverse St. Louisans can plan for a future in which the city can again claim a solid position—this time on the global, not just American, stage.

—Anna E. Crosslin

Anna E. Crosslin has served as president & CEO of the International Institute of St. Louis since 1978. Founded in 1919, the Institute, a private charitable organization, is rooted in the national settlement house movement ". . . to integrate war refugees into the American mainstream by promoting ethnic identity and leadership, being inclusive, and teaching Democracy and self-reliance." Members of nearly every immigrant community arriving in St. Louis in the past 100 years have benefited from the Institute's integrative services and cultural programs. Today, the Institute is St. Louis's Welcome Center for thousands of immigrants and refugees as they seek to establish new lives in the St. Louis region and also sponsors the popular annual Festival of Nations.

ORIGINS

The first forty or so years of its existence placed St. Louis on the map as a prosperous, multiethnic village. The French leaders established a thriving fur commerce based on the laissez-faire policies of the ruling Spanish and friendship with the surrounding Osage Indians. The community capitalized on trade upriver with French Canada, downriver with New Orleans, and across the river with America, setting St. Louis apart as a commercial hub. These successes were threatened with the Louisiana Purchase.

BY 1860 ST. LOUIS WAS THE MOST FOREIGN-BORN CITY IN THE NATION

American rule began the breakdown of Indian relations and their eventual forced retreat. River commerce soon included a brutal slave trade. The fur trade dissipated and the French community lost its strength. From the 1840s through the 1860s, Irish and German immigrants flooded into the city. St. Louis was at first ill-prepared for the massive influx of immigrants. "By 1850, 43 percent of all St. Louisans were born in either Ireland or Germany." Other Europeans followed, and by 1860 St. Louis was the most foreign-born city in the nation. With this influx came poverty, crime, and violence. As St. Louis adjusted, the contributions of the new citizens made the Gateway City a beacon for new immigrants. Later waves of settlers included Italians, Serbians, Lebanese, Syrians, and Greeks. By the 1890s, St. Louis was the nation's fourth-largest city.

Native American

Pierre de Laclède's new village, St. Louis, received these visitors only months after he had founded the settlement. Townsfolk were set on edge as the entire Missouria tribe, 400 to 600 strong, filed into the town and made plans to build a permanent encampment around Laclède's house. The Missouria nation, weakened by European disease and hunger, wished to stay in St. Louis because they feared their Indian enemies. Laclède exercised his power of diplomacy and suggested they move on, lest their Indian enemies attack St. Louis, endangering his fellow Frenchmen. Lacking enough food and provisions to send the Missouria satisfactorily on their way, Laclède sent for food from Cahokia.

While the Indians waited the fifteen or so days for their food, young Auguste Chouteau employed the Missouria women and children in various chores, including digging and moving dirt for the construction of Laclède's large house and company building. The walls of that structure witnessed many councils between the people of the regional Indian nations, the Spanish government, and the French people of St. Louis for years after. As author Michael Dickey noted, "Missouria women and children literally helped lay the foundations of St. Louis."

The relationship between the St. Louis French and the surrounding Indians, especially the powerful Osage, was rooted in the fur trade. Pierre de Laclède and brothers Auguste and Pierre Chouteau immersed themselves in Osage culture, often living among them.

During the 1770s and 1780s, the fur trade in St. Louis was lucrative; Indians flocked to St. Louis, traded their furs with local merchants, and received presents from the Spanish government.

Interconnected relationships emerged. As it was customary among the Osage to offer women of status to non-Osage men to solidify business transactions, this practice often resulted in mixed-blood children, called *métis*. The Chouteau brothers took "country wives" of the Osage women, even though they had French wives in St. Louis. French traders often brought their Indian children to St. Louis to be baptized according to the French Catholic customs. St. Louis citizens saw regional Indians walk their streets as neighbors, trading partners, occasional antagonists, and slaves.

During the American Revolution, St. Louis was attacked by British troops and nearly one thousand warriors of their Indian allies. Those included the Sauks and Mesquakies, longtime traders in St. Louis. The skirmish lasted only hours, largely because the Indians were frightened by the Spanish artillery.

After the war, the Americans on the east side of the Mississippi River competed with St. Louisans for trading rights with the local Indians. In 1787, the Spanish government banned trade with the Osage as a result of difficult relations with the tribe. Accordingly, the profitability of the fur trade declined in the 1790s. The Chouteaus appeased the officials by building nearby forts to be used specifically for trading purposes. The forts eased tension by diminishing the heavy trading traffic within the village of St. Louis.

When France sold the Louisiana Territory to the United States in 1803, Pierre Chouteau led a contingent of Osage from St. Louis to Washington, D.C., to meet their new "father," Thomas Jefferson. The Indians were as awed by American cities as the people of the East were by the display of the Osage in their native dress. A second group followed in 1805–1806. This time, chiefs from twelve nations gathered in St. Louis for the trip, including Osage, Sioux, Sac and Fox, Kansa, and Iowa.

Except for the *métis*, the Indian presence declined in St. Louis during the following decades. Weakened by European diseases such as smallpox, the scourge of alcohol, and warfare with Indians based on European alliances, the tribes' numbers dwindled. Americans were different from the French and the Spanish in that they wanted land to farm. Once-great Indian nations signed treaty after treaty, surrendering large swaths of land to the American government in return for allowances and reservation land in the West. The proud Osage returned once again to St. Louis in 1904, but only as a spectacle at the World's Fair.

By the mid-nineteenth century, St. Louis bustled as an American city. It no longer served as the central location for trade, peace councils, and expeditions in which the Native Americans played a central role. Sugar Loaf Mound, the still-standing monument of the Mississippian culture on today's Ohio Street in south St. Louis, is the property of the Osage Nation, now of Oklahoma.

Once per year, Washington University comes alive with a multi-tribal powwow, complete with the cultural costumes, dances, drums, songs, and deep spirit of their ancestors. Otherwise, there are few reminders in St. Louis of the Native American people who walked these streets. But remember this: "in some respects, Missouria women and children literally helped lay the foundations of St. Louis."

French

The legend of Pierre de Laclède's navigation up the Mississippi River in search of the perfect spot to establish a trading post is a romantic notion in St. Louis history. In reality, the Frenchman rowed a keelboat, maneuvering through the angry currents of the untamed river, often while being towed by thirty brawny boatmen who fought muck, tree snags, mosquitoes, snakes, and the threat of Indian attacks along the river's edge. But he made it. In December 1763, Laclède selected a bluff below the confluence of the Missouri and the Mississippi Rivers. The site was then in Spanish territory and is now home to the Gateway Arch.

After choosing the site for his trading post, Laclède and his entourage weathered the worst of the winter at Fort de Chartres, near the river in French Illinois. In February 1764, Laclède remained at the fort with the supplies and sent fourteen-year-old Auguste Chouteau to establish St. Louis, named for King Louis IX of France. Chouteau oversaw the felling of trees and the erection of the first structures. Laclède arrived in April with the provisions. Laclède had landed.

St. Louis quickly began to take shape. Buildings spread out across the hill, with a few streets and cross streets. The frontier town consisted of large lots for houses, barns, and gardens. The village's population was boosted by French families who moved across the river, leaving behind the Illinois that France ceded to Great Britain in the 1763 Treaty of Paris. These French

leaders. Together they advanced Laclède's directive, supervising the activity of the village, befriending the local Indians, and managing the flourishing trade of furs exploited from the vast frontier of the West.

In 1800, by a secret treaty whose terms became known only later, Spain returned the Louisiana Territory to France. Three years later, France sold the Louisiana Territory to the United States. Over the next two decades the St. Louis French community adapted to American customs. Their ideals of reconciliation and a communal property system gave way to the common law of the American legal system. Their mercantilist society transformed into a capitalistic society, and American Protestants steadily joined their Catholic community.

The "first families" of St. Louis, prosperous from the successful early years of the fur trade, retreated. "Frenchtown" began as country residences for those city merchants. The elite French families of St. Louis built estates that stretched from Carondelet Road to the river, and from Chouteau's Pond (the low land of the rail yard and parking lots south of Busch Stadium) to Sugar Loaf Mound. There, the aristocratic men and women who encompassed the spirit on which St. Louis was built spoke French with one another and continued to contribute to the growth of the community.

Antoine Soulard left France during the French Revolution. He made his way to St. Louis thirty years after the city's founding and was awarded land near

settlers of St. Louis, historically referred to as French, Creole, and French Creole, were men and women of French ancestry who, in their new homeland, developed their own culture and their own French dialect.

Laclède, who maintained a good relationship with the Spanish government, possessed sole rights to trade with the Indian nations located west of the Mississippi River for eight years. His trading post quickly became a thriving enterprise. Auguste Chouteau and his brother Jean Pierre Chouteau proved themselves fine village

Carondelet Road for his duties as a surveyor for Upper Louisiana. Soulard, along with Charles Gratiot, was among the signatories of the document that officially relinquished the Louisiana Territory to the United States. After his death in 1825, his widow, Julia, built a beautiful home in Frenchtown. In 1838, she designated two city blocks to be used as a public market. In so doing, she established Soulard Market, as well as the neighborhood now known as Soulard.

Today, a new thriving French community exists in St. Louis. The St. Louis–Lyon, France, sister city affiliation was formed in 1976 and has been active since. The Alliance Française de St. Louis is an organization that promotes French language and culture. This association, located on Delmar Boulevard, is St. Louis's contemporary branch of the Parisian organization founded in 1883. And for a taste of France, French cuisine is abundant in St. Louis's bistros and cafes.

Though Frenchtown is no longer a St. Louis neighborhood, the early French influence on the city remains. Street names and neighborhoods honor the original founders and early society leaders of St. Louis. And legendary events such as the Big Muddy Blues Festival and Rockin' on the Landing on Independence Day make Laclede's Landing just as relevant as it was in 1764.

Spanish

Pierre de Laclède had not yet established his trading post on the bluff below the confluence of the Missouri and Mississippi Rivers when, on November 13, 1762, Spain took possession of the territory of Louisiana from France through the Treaty of Fontainebleau. The little French village of St. Louis likely first learned that it was under Spanish governance in early 1765, a year after its founding in 1764 and three years after the treaty was signed.

St. Louisans signed an oath of allegiance to Spain in 1769, and the first permanent Spanish lieutenant governor arrived in St. Louis in 1770. Though St. Louis was the official capital of governance for the upper portion of the territory, the hub of the Spanish government remained in New Orleans. The Spanish authority in St. Louis was relegated to a small, ineffective contingent of Spanish commandants. The positive relationship between the townspeople of St. Louis and the Spanish officials was due to the capable leadership of the advisor to the Spanish, Louis St. Ange de Bellerive. Though he was French, Spanish authorities appointed Bellerive as captain in the Spanish militia. St. Louis citizens largely governed themselves. Essentially, St. Louis remained French in custom, language, Catholicism, and life.

The Spanish fortified St. Louis with artillery, fending off a British and Indian attack during the American Revolution. The successful French relations with the Osage Indians were threatened in the 1790s when the Spanish government banned trade with the Osage Nation, whom they viewed as increasingly hostile. The only notable Spanish traders in the region at the time were Benito Vásquez and the strong-willed Manuel Lisa. The St. Louisans pacified their Spanish authorities by building a fort nearby, exclusively for trade outside St. Louis proper.

In 1800, Napoleon forced Spain to give the Louisiana Territory to France with the secret Treaty of San Ildefonso. Four short years later, St. Louisans raised the American flag. A two-part ceremony in St. Louis marked the transfer of the territory. On March 9, 1804, the lieutenant governor of Spain signed the document that legitimately surrendered Upper Louisiana to France. This was necessary as France had not publicly assumed control four years earlier. The next day, the United States officially purchased the territory from France. This was the last involvement of the Spanish government in colonial St. Louis.

The Spanish reappeared in St. Louis in the early twentieth century. Drawn by employment at the Edgar Zinc Company on Blow Street near the railroad tracks, most of the first Spanish immigrants came from the Asturias region of Spain, home to zinc mines. These newcomers settled in "Spanish Town" in the Carondelet neighborhood. The area, from the 6900 block to the 7300 block between South Broadway and Minnesota Avenue, became home for the Spaniards who worked in the zinc smelter.

The St. Louis Spanish Benevolent Society was created in 1908 to ease the transition from Spain to America. As the Spanish assimilated into St. Louis, the children of Spanish Town attended Blow School. The Jesuit priests of St. Louis recognized the growing number of Spanish-speaking families and began a Catholic Spanish mission in 1912. The parish was officially organized in 1915, led by Father Jose Pico of Mexico, and families attended Our Lady of Covadonga Church at 7100 Virginia Avenue. Father Jose Pico left in 1920, but the church continued on until it closed in 1932. Spanish Town fielded a soccer team named Asturias for their home region, playing their games at Mannion's Field at 8600 South Broadway. There, they won divisional titles in 1914 and 1931 in the Municipal Soccer League.

As the twentieth century marched onward, citizens of Spanish Town moved on. But the Spanish Society, at the same location since 1908, continued to thrive, with its membership peaking in the 1940s and 1950s. Inside these walls at 7107 Michigan Avenue, the Spanish of St. Louis attended dances, formed ladies' auxiliaries and children's clubs, and imbibed at the society's tavern. And still today, with all the color and spirit of a fiesta, the Spanish Society is a beacon to St. Louis's Spanish past and present.

Swiss

Swiss heritage in St. Louis dates as far back as the city's founding years. Charles Gratiot was born in Switzerland and educated in England. After first traveling to Montreal in 1769, Gratiot moved to Cahokia in British Illinois territory, and opened a store in 1777. At the invitation of Auguste Chouteau, Gratiot, a Huguenot, moved to Catholic St. Louis. In 1781, he married the youngest of Madame Chouteau's daughters. His marriage solidified his status as an important fixture in the early years of St. Louis.

In the mid-nineteenth century, the Swiss began to immigrate to St. Louis. The *Missouri Republican* reported in 1844, "The steamer *Ben Franklin*, from New Orleans, brought up 133 Swiss emigrants, bound for the upper part of the Missouri River . . . in port for St. Louis." In 1857, the *Missouri Republican* noted, "several hundred members of a Swiss colony who have arrived in this city, held a meeting yesterday, and determined to settle in Missouri." The Swiss immigrants' destinations were often farmland. Many, though, stayed in St. Louis. There were enough Swiss in St. Louis in 1849 to form the Gruetli Verein, a benevolent society, to help transition new Swiss immigrants to their St. Louis home.

By 1880, more than two thousand ethnic Swiss lived in St. Louis. The steady arrival of Swiss immigrants continued through the turn of the century. The Gruetli Verein, still going strong in 1910, changed its name to the Schweizer Bund.

There were not enough Swiss immigrants to form a cohesive, geographic enclave in St. Louis like some ethnic groups—they lived all around the city. Emigration from Switzerland abated through the remainder of the twentieth century. Though the Swiss community in St. Louis is quiet today, their legacy is a permanent imprint on the history of St. Louis.

African American

From the earliest days of its founding, St. Louis has been home to African Americans. The 1799 census reported that African Americans made up more than a third of the city's population, with 56 free blacks, 268 slaves, and 601 whites. Meriwether Lewis and William Clark returned to St. Louis in 1806 from their famous expedition, having been accompanied by York, Clark's slave. York, the only African American on the expedition, proved an invaluable asset to the explorers and their mission.

The first African American church was founded in St. Louis in 1835, and it served as a social center for the black community, both enslaved and free. Even with the 1847 law against educating blacks in the state of Missouri, they managed to teach their children in church basements and in a steamboat on the Mississippi River, officially outside state lines.

Despite a growing national abolitionist fervor, St. Louis thrived as a slave auction center. Enslaved men, women, and children stood on the east steps of the Old Courthouse while their lives were sold. Others were sold by traders Corbin and Thompson, who operated on 6th Street, between Pine and Chestnut. Lynch's auction house stood on Locust Street, the current site of the Federal Reserve Bank, with slave pens on Broadway, next to today's Busch Stadium.

Fugitive slave laws grew harsher, yet freedom in Illinois, a non-slave state, beckoned. The Mary Meachum Freedom Crossing site in north St. Louis provided one such dangerous opportunity. At the Mississippi River ferry crossing in 1855, about eight slaves rowed toward freedom, aided by a free man and Mary Meachum, widow of the founder of the First African Baptist Church of St. Louis. Five of those slaves were apprehended, some of whom were the property of Henry Shaw, founder of the Missouri Botanical Garden. They were punished severely. One, Esther, was sold downriver and her children were sold away from her.

Slavery in urban St. Louis was unique, compared to the isolation of a plantation. By the 1850s, slave ownership had become less profitable in St. Louis. Irish and German immigrants flooded the city, making up 43 percent of the population and providing cheap labor that made slave labor economically less necessary. Owners hired out their slaves, who were often allowed to keep a small portion of the wage. Some slaves hired themselves out on Sundays. As a result, there was a fairly large free slave population in St. Louis, a small number of whom petitioned for and purchased their freedom. Free African Americans ("free" being a relative term) owned real estate, worked as laborers unloading cargo off steamboats, and owned "barber emporiums," often patronized by wealthy whites. A small class of "black aristocracy" emerged in antebellum St. Louis.

The famous freedom suit case in St. Louis involved Dred and Harriet Scott. For nine years, Scott lived in free territories with the man who purchased him in St. Louis, Dr. John Emerson. After Emerson's death and upon their return to St. Louis, the widow Emerson hired out the Scott family. It was then, in 1847, that fifty-year-old Dred Scott sued for his freedom. A series of trials and appeals, most in St. Louis's Old Courthouse, culminated in the United States Supreme Court ruling that freedom laws were less important than property laws, denying the Scotts their freedom. Despite the loss, the lawsuit raised awareness for basic human rights.

Years after emancipation, life was increasingly oppressive in the rural South. Great numbers of African Americans moved northward. First, exodusters (a name given to African Americans who migrated from states along the Mississippi River to Kansas in the late nineteenth century) moved through St. Louis, seeking rural land in Kansas and the West. The Great Migration of the early twentieth century filled St. Louis and other cities with African Americans in search of factory work. Between 1900 and 1940, St. Louis's black population nearly tripled.

Racial discrimination—first social, then legal— restricted housing options for blacks in St. Louis. Neighborhoods where blacks were allowed to live, like the Ville in north St. Louis, were the poorest and oldest sections of the city. As a result, African Americans suffered from extremely overcrowded conditions and the consequences of living in squalor. The 1948 United

States Supreme Court decision in *Shelley v. Kraemer* ruled in favor of the African American Shelley family, securing their right to purchase a home in Lewis Place, a white St. Louis neighborhood that runs from Walton to Taylor, between Newberry Terrace and MacMillan Avenue. This brave purchase slowly moved St. Louis blacks in the direction of housing fairness.

In spite of the discrimination, African American families in St. Louis worked, played, and raised their families. Annie Malone invented and successfully sold her hair care products. Black St. Louisans fielded two Negro League baseball teams. And St. Louis was the center of ragtime music in the early twentieth century. Black entertainment districts, near Union Station and in the heavily populated Mill Creek Valley neighborhood, offered ragtime venues. The King of Rag, Scott Joplin, wrote "The Entertainer" while living on Delmar Boulevard. African American St. Louisans lived through the indignity of segregation—separate but certainly not equal. In spite of the grossly inadequate resources provided them, black doctors healed the sick at Homer G. Phillips Hospital, and black St. Louisans educated their young at two all-black high schools, Sumner and Vashon. Music icons Chuck Berry and Tina Turner, and boxer Leon Spinks are among the many notable graduates of the schools.

The Civil Rights Movement in St. Louis coincided with such activities in cities around the country. Protests, sit-ins, and demonstrations marked the fight for racial equality in mid-twentieth-century St. Louis. African Americans utilized the strength of the National Association for the Advancement of Colored People (NAACP), established the Congress of Racial Equality (CORE), and formed the St. Louis Black Liberators. Such greats as Martin Luther King Jr. paid a visit to St. Louis, and challenges to racial equality were met with protests, both peaceful and violent.

Notable protests and lawsuits marked slow but steady progress toward racial justice. In 1938, the United States Supreme Court ruled that the University of Missouri must admit black students to its law school, or create a separate but equal law school for Lloyd Gaines and future black students. In 1963, African Americans demonstrated at the Jefferson Bank on Washington and Jefferson Streets, protesting the lack of black employees in downtown businesses. A year later, Percy Green and Richard Daly scaled the unfinished legs of the Gateway Arch to protest the whites-only job site. In 1971, the U.S. Federal Court of Appeals cited the fair housing rule from the 1968 Civil Rights Act in a ruling against the community of Black Jack. A year later, Minnie Liddell filed a lawsuit against the St. Louis Board of Education, leading to desegregation of the St. Louis public schools.

African Americans comprise the only ethnic group that has lived in St. Louis from the first Creoles until today. The journey of these African Americans is a complex dichotomy of pain and healing, defeat and triumph, and ultimately, strength. While racial harmony is an ongoing process, today's African Americans in St. Louis stand tall on the shoulders of those generations before them.

GROWTH AS A MULTIETHNIC CITY: 1800s

JEWISH

In 1807, just four years after the United States purchased the Louisiana Territory from France, Jewish immigrant Joseph Philipson opened a store in St. Louis with his brother Jacob. Wolf Bloch, a Jewish native of Bohemia, settled in St. Louis in 1816, followed by Eleazer Bloch in 1817. The Jewish population in St. Louis grew steadily through the nineteenth century. By 1850, nearly one thousand Jews lived in the city.

In the mid-nineteenth century, the Jewish community in St. Louis actively established their religious centers. In 1836, ten men met in a room above a grocery store at the corner of 2nd and Spruce Streets, holding Jewish services. In 1841, that group organized into their first congregation, United Hebrew, which is still in existence. The B'nai El congregation organized in 1840 and built their first temple at 6th and Cerre Streets in 1855. In 1847, the Emanu El congregation, made up largely of German Jews, first met over a livery stable on 5th Street. Two years later, Bohemian Jews formed B'nai B'rith, meeting in south St. Louis at Fulton and Lafayette. In 1852, Emanu El and B'nai B'rith merged to form B'nai El, as a cholera epidemic depleted memberships in both. The Shaare Emeth congregation was established in 1866, and from this congregation members left to organize Temple Israel in 1886. In 1878, the oldest existing Orthodox synagogue in St. Louis, Beth Hamedrosh Hagodol, was founded. This synagogue continues to serve Jews in University City today.

Along with their houses of worship, St. Louis Jews prepared places for their dead. The first Jewish cemetery, Mount Olive, was established in 1844. The B'nai El congregation purchased their cemetery, Mount Sinai, on Gravois Road in 1849. The Beth Hamedrosh Hagodol *shul* (or synagogue) in University City also has a cemetery. Other cemeteries around St. Louis, such as the historic Bellefontaine Cemetery, provide eternal homes for various religious and ethnic populations, including Jews.

Great waves of eastern European Jews immigrated to St. Louis toward the end of the nineteenth century. In 1880, the Jewish community numbered around ten thousand, and by 1900 that number reached forty thousand. Worship centers continued to sprout up in the city. The conservative B'nai Amoona congregation was founded in 1881. Temple Israel was built at 28th and Pine in 1888, and Russian Jewish immigrants founded the Chesed Shel Emeth Society that same year. Their Orthodox cemetery was established in 1893 at Olive and Hanley. By 1905, St. Louis was home to six Orthodox synagogues.

Like most Jewish communities around the nation, the St. Louis Jewish community faced discrimination—some overt, some that smoldered just below the surface. This negativity became more apparent toward the turn of the twentieth century. Documented discrimination includes employment, housing, and recreation, including everything from swimming pools to resorts. The next uptick in outward anti-Semitism occurred as the United States progressed into World War II. This led to the creation of groups like the Jewish Community Relations Council (JCRC), which continues to work to bring together and educate the St. Louis region, with the goal of stopping discrimination of all kinds. Unfortunately, St. Louis served as a hub for various extremists and hate groups throughout the twentieth century, including headquarters for anti-Semitic leader Gerald L. K. Smith.

The St. Louis Jewish community persevered. Lodges, clubs, philanthropic organizations, and charitable societies sprang up to benefit members of the Jewish population in St. Louis. In turn, these organizations helped unify the Jewish community, whose members heralded from varying homelands, embraced differing traditions, and spoke multiple languages. Many of these organizations remain today. The Jewish Alliance of America was founded in the 1890s to assist eastern European Jews in transitioning to life in St. Louis. Over time, the alliance merged with other benevolent societies, resulting in the Jewish Federation of St. Louis in the 1920s. Today the Jewish Federation oversees twenty charitable organizations designed to aid both the Jewish and non-Jewish populations in the St. Louis area. The Young Men's Hebrew Association, founded in 1880, and the Young Women's Hebrew Association eventually evolved into the Jewish Community Center, now located in Creve Coeur and popularly referred to as "the J." Schools and newspapers further unified the St. Louis Jewish community through the generations.

Additionally, notable Jewish men and women played important roles in St. Louis history—their landmarks stand as a testament to their contributions. These include the Nathan Frank Bandstand, located in

front of the Muny. Frank was the founder of the *St. Louis Star* and also served in the U.S. Congress. The Central Institute for the Deaf, 825 South Taylor Avenue, was founded in 1914 by Dr. Max A. Goldstein, a pioneer in identifying variations in deafness and deaf education. Tilles Park, at McKnight and Litzsinger Roads, was once the private estate of Jewish philanthropist C. A. Tilles. Aloe Plaza, across from Union Station, was built in memory of city leader Louis P. Aloe. The Bertha Guggenheim Memorial Fountain at the Muny was erected in 1918, recognizing a leader of the women's suffrage campaign in Missouri. Jewish Hospital was built with funds raised by the St. Louis Jewish community in 1902. They opened their Kingshighway location in 1927 and merged with Barnes Hospital in 1996. These and many other landmarks in St. Louis proudly represent the vibrant St. Louis Jewish community.

German

Germans first began to settle in St. Louis in significant numbers in the 1830s. Life in the fatherland had grown increasingly intolerable because of overpopulation and poverty, as well as economic, social, and political upheaval. Many were motivated to immigrate by the notion of creating a new Germany, or a better version of the original, in Missouri. In 1835, there were enough Germans in St. Louis to found the first German newspaper, the *Anzeiger des Westens*. Two years later, a German school opened, even before the city established its first public school.

The failed Revolution of 1848 was the catalyst for a massive wave of German immigration. Soon, the quiet French village on the confluence of the Missouri and Mississippi Rivers was teeming with this new population who spoke German, filled tenement houses, and brewed beer. By 1853, the city of St. Louis boasted six German newspapers and seven German societies.

Nativism reared its ugly head during the 1850s, and the newly arrived Germans clashed with anti-immigrant rioters. St. Louis Germans detested slavery, and many fought bravely during the Civil War. Despite the unrest, the German immigrants settled into the fabric of St. Louis. Many found employment in the brewing industry, of which fellow Germans William Lemp and Adolphus Busch were icons.

The brick towers of both men's breweries stand proudly in St. Louis's south side. While Prohibition snuffed out Lemp's brewery, the fragrance of hops still swirls around Anheuser-Busch today. The Busch name is synonymous with St. Louis: founder Adolphus built the beer empire, son August survived Prohibition, and grandson Gussie ushered the King of Beers into the world market. Though they've relinquished Anheuser-Busch to InBev, this well-known German American family's legacy can be experienced through brunch at Bevo Mill, the wonder of the Clydesdales at Grant's Farm, and the roar of the crowd at Busch Stadium.

The Germans brought sacred pieces of their heritage to St. Louis. They stayed true to cultural customs like eating sauerkraut and bratwurst. Beer gardens, where German families gathered on Sundays, became the cherished tradition in St. Louis that it was back in Germany. And hallowed institutions, like the turnverein movement, found their way to St. Louis. The first turnverein, or gymnastic society, west of the Mississippi River was organized in St. Louis in 1850. Five years later, the St. Louis Turnverein occupied a grand building on 10th Street between Market and Walnut. The Concordia Turner Hall on Gravois is the last of fourteen turnvereins in St. Louis.

The Civil War incited passion among the German immigrants, who left their own country as a result of infractions on their liberties. Many fought honorably for the Union, most notably in the defense of the St. Louis Arsenal and in the capture of pro-Confederate Camp Jackson. The site of Camp Jackson is part of the present-day campus of Saint Louis University.

As St. Louis grew, it developed north and south along the river, and later west. German immigrants

organized verein (societies), attended churches, and patronized saloons in their own neighborhoods. Germans established neighborhoods as far south as Carondelet. They settled in north St. Louis neighborhoods such as Hyde Park and in what later became the Italian enclave known as the Hill. The Hyde Park area, founded by Emil Mallinckrodt, was first called Bremen after a city in northern Germany. New immigrants felt at home in Bremen, which mirrored a native German town.

The German American population of St. Louis came together to proudly represent themselves during the 1904 World's Fair, although World War I and Prohibition ushered in an era of anti-German sentiment. As the twentieth century progressed, German Americans saw their cultural centers fade—but they are far from gone. The German School Association of Greater St. Louis currently teaches German language and culture in south St. Louis. The German Cultural Society boasts an excellent oompa band. And St. Louisans of every heritage flock to Soulard for the annual Oktoberfest.

Hallmarks of the German contribution to the narrative of St. Louis history are everywhere. And celebrated German immigrants, such as Heinrich Bornstein, editor of the *Anzeiger des Westens*; Carl Wimar, known for his paintings of American Indians; and longtime, unscrupulous St. Louis mayor Henry Kiel are only a few of the many German immigrants who added concrete to the foundation on which St. Louis stands today.

English, Scottish, and Welsh

St. Louis historian James Neal Primm writes, "Of sixty-eight families who came to St. Louis between 1804 and 1816, one each [came from] Scotland and Wales." The St. Louis suburb Manchester was named after a resident's hometown in England. Immigrants from England, Scotland, and Wales have been in the St. Louis region since the Louisiana Purchase.

These immigrant groups did not arrive in great waves, but enough made their way to St. Louis during the nineteenth century to establish a community. By 1870, 1,341 Scottish immigrants and around 350 Welsh called St. Louis their home. The 1880 census listed 8,762 English residents.

These immigrants from Great Britain worked, played, and worshipped. Many found employment in the south St. Louis clay mines. They, especially the Scots, contributed to the establishment of soccer, building the foundation for generations of soccer leagues in St. Louis. Though the Welsh didn't construct a church building, they formed their own congregation, meeting in a rented room, worshipping with Calvinist Methodist and Wesleyan preachers.

The Scottish immigrants, however, built a church. The members of St. Margaret of Scotland Catholic Church first held services in a vacant storefront at the corner of Russell Boulevard and 39th Street in 1900. The parish then built a beautiful church at 3854 Flad Avenue in 1906, where the church continues to thrive today. St. Margaret of Scotland Parish School was

built in 1918 at Lawrence and Castleman in the Shaw neighborhood of south St. Louis and has educated St. Louis children since.

The St. Louis branch of the English-Speaking Union of the United States (ESU) was established in 1920, founded "in no narrow attitude of race pride, in no spirit of hostility to any people." The organization operates on an educational mission, with activities that include the National Shakespeare Competition, a scholarship program, and a speaker program. Additionally, the ESU provides the British Universities Summer School Fellowships, in which high school teachers study at prestigious British centers of learning, including Oxford University.

Equally active is the Daughters of the British Empire in Missouri. Based in St. Louis, this organization boasts branches around the state and country. This

philanthropic organization, which supports local charities, was founded in Missouri in 1946 and still touts its motto: "Not Ourselves but the Cause."

St. Louisans of Scottish ethnicity are vibrantly visible. The Scottish St. Andrew Society was founded in 1972, and today it remains dedicated to its objective of encompassing historical, educational, cultural, charitable, and philanthropic activities to further the exchange between those of Scottish heritage and St. Louis. Be sure to gather your clan and head over to Forest Park for the annual Scottish games, which include sword fighting, bagpiping, and folk dancing fun.

Irish

The kids love the brightly colored floats and the huge inflatables. The moms and dads love the free entertainment and the impressive marching bands. And a lot of people love the early taste of spring and the robust taste of beer. But it's likely that few people at the annual St. Patrick's Day parades in St. Louis consider the important contribution of the Irish to the history of the city.

The Irish immigrated to St. Louis in two waves. The earliest group arrived in St. Louis soon after the Louisiana Purchase opened up the West, from 1804 until the 1830s. St. Louis was a burgeoning center of commerce for the country's midsection, and the city became a beacon for Irish businessmen weary of their country's economic oppression by the English. Further, the French residents of St. Louis welcomed the Irish, as opposed to the discrimination shown by those in eastern cities. Most of the French shared the Irishmen's Catholic faith. And those early Irish newcomers proved themselves worthy of the hospitality.

They arrived in St. Louis ready to better themselves, their city, and the lives of those who followed. Irishman Joseph Charless began the first newspaper west of the Mississippi River. Businessman John Mullanphy reigned as a real estate king. His properties along the Mississippi River Valley catapulted him to multimillionaire status. Mullanphy, along with fellow Ireland natives John O'Fallon and Jeremiah Connor, donated land and money to Saint Louis College (now Saint Louis University). They deeded land to the city, including Washington Avenue, and they built hospitals, orphanages, and benevolent societies. By the 1830s, one in seven St. Louisans were Irish immigrants, and these men and women were well-respected members of St. Louis society.

The 1840s brought the second wave of Irish immigrants to St. Louis. Economic oppression and the Irish potato famine contributed to the race for America. Unlike the immigrating Germans and British, who generally brought money and purchased land, the second wave of Irish were poor. Their vast numbers alarmed the "native" St. Louisans, even the early Irish settlers. This gave rise to movements such as the anti-immigrant Know-Nothings, which essentially meant anti–everything Irish: their poverty, their customs, and their Catholicism.

The inhospitable environment made housing an impossibility, so the Irish immigrants squatted on open land on the near north side of St. Louis. They built shanties, and this impoverished section of town became known as Kerry Patch. Children played in the streets amongst the hovels and taverns. Kerry Patch became a haven of Irish culture and pride as well as gang violence. St. Lawrence O'Toole Church was first established in 1855 at 14th and O'Fallon Streets. Its parishioners built a gorgeous new building in 1864 dubbed the "Pride of the Patch." Kerry Patch's geographic boundaries are historically ambiguous, but their neighborhood center originated first on 14th

Street, then migrated west between Biddle Street and Cass Avenue, and finally moved to 18th Street during the 1880s.

Cheltenham, another Irish enclave, centered around today's intersection of Manchester Road and Hampton Avenue in the present-day Dogtown neighborhood. Many of these residents worked in nearby clay mines. The neighborhood church, St. James the Greater Parish, was led by Father John O'Sullivan, an Irish priest. St. James was built in 1861 at 1368 Tamm Avenue. In contrast to the social and financial struggles of their parents, the American-born children of the Irish immigrants enjoyed an easier life. By the 1920s, the tightly knit, impoverished Irish communities had scattered into the wind, their former residents strengthened by assimilation and improved economic circumstances.

Irish-born John J. Glennon served as archbishop of the Catholic Church from 1903 to 1946. Known for reaching the masses with his commanding presence and oratory skills, Archbishop Glennon outwardly opposed women's suffrage and the integration of

blacks. Yet his dream for opening a health care facility for all children was realized in 1956, ten years after his death in his native Ireland. SSM Cardinal Glennon Children's Medical Center, on South Grand, provides top-notch medical care for children from around the world.

For those seeking a refined introduction to Irish culture, consider a music or dance class at the St. Louis Irish Arts. Of course, there's always St. Patrick's Day festivities. The first St. Patrick's Day celebration in St. Louis was held in 1820. The revelries continue, whether it's at the family-friendly St. Patrick's Day parade on Market Street or the more wide-open event in Dogtown. The legacy of the St. Louis Irish lives on.

THE ITALIAN IMMIGRANTS

Italian

Compared with their eventual impact, the Italian community in St. Louis started small. In 1848, about fifty Italian immigrants lived in the city. By the 1860s, the St. Louis Italians were six hundred strong. Most came from the Genoa province of Italy, occupying the area from the levee to 12th Street and from Franklin Avenue to Spruce Street. As the turn of the century approached, Sicilians moved into the near north side area of 7th and Carr. "Little Italy" became home to these new inhabitants, who filled up tenements alongside members of other ethnic groups, from 6th Street west to 12th Street and from Franklin Avenue to Cass Avenue. These new immigrants settled into city life, with the men often working in the clay mines and the women often working in the garment district.

In the late nineteenth century, peasants in the Lombardy region of northern Italy faced a dismal future within a feudal system. They saw opportunity in the industrialization of the United States. Between 1880 and 1900, many immigrated to America to work in the clay mines and brick factories of St. Louis. They found work at the Evens and Howard clay pits, Laclede Fire Brick Works, Cheltenham Fire Brick Works, and in brick kilns on the banks of the River des Peres. These Italian immigrants built their shacks on an uninhabited hill southwest of the city. Then they brought over their families.

Life was hard for these first-generation Italians who settled on the Hill. But with a network of friends and families from the old country, the Hill became a tightly knit community. Italians from Sicily, the minority, showed reciprocal prejudice with the Lombards. But by the 1920s and 1930s, the second generation placed more importance on their local neighborhood gangs than the ethnicity of their parents. Their parents' work ethic had transformed the Hill from rows of shacks to rows of tidy bungalows. The Hill's first school, Shaw School, was initially located on Kingshighway and Vandeventer in 1870, but moved to 5329 Columbia Avenue in 1907. St. Ambrose Church was built in 1903 at 2110 Cooper Street. This impressive building, constructed by Italian hands from bricks of St. Louis clay and fired in kilns on the Hill, became a cornerstone of the community.

The Italian Americans living in the Little Italy neighborhood attended Our Lady Help of Christians Church at 1010 Cole Street and St. Charles Borromeo Church on 29th and Locust Streets. Both churches were organized in 1900. Their children went to school at Patrick Henry School on 12th and 10th Streets, and their social groups included the Little Italy drum corps. By the 1920s, some in the Italian American community became involved in organized crime, a side effect of Prohibition. Likewise, many residents of the Hill became bootleggers. But the values and cohesiveness of the community helped to isolate the neighborhood from the violence plaguing the city.

Athletics transformed America in the 1920s and 1930s. The first playground on the Hill was built in 1924 at Shaw School. Sports clubs sprang up through St. Ambrose Church, the Y.M.C.A., and on neighborhood street corners. Youth played soccer, softball, baseball, and other competitive sports at the Fairmount Playground on the corner of Boardman and Shaw, and at Foundry Field at Kingshighway and Southwest Avenue. Later, Vigo Park on Macklind Avenue, renamed Berra Park, became one of the Hill's most treasured playing fields. Baseball greats Joe Garagiola and Lawrence "Yogi" Berra lived on the same block on the Hill.

World War II transformed the isolated Hill community. Young men and women ventured out of the confines of the neighborhood to serve their country. Many married and moved off the Hill. However, the soul of the enclave, once exclusively Italian, remains. Ubiquitous Italian flags and restaurants like Charlie Gitto's, Dominic's, Giovanni's, and Cunetto's attest to the longevity and Italian flavor of the Hill.

Serbian

The timeline of the Holy Trinity Serbian Orthodox Church reflects the ethnic complexity and immigration patterns of the St. Louis Serbian community. Serbian immigrants were documented as living in St. Louis as early as 1881. When they first settled in St. Louis, they grouped together according to the Serbian region from which they hailed. One enclave lived on North Broadway, another on Chouteau Avenue, and a third in South City. Regardless of their roots, the Serbs joined together to create their new church in 1909.

The congregation purchased a three-story building on 8th and Barry Streets in 1911. There they established a church, school, and social hall. The congregation worshipped with Russian, Bulgarian, and Greek Orthodox priests until they found a Serbian priest for their new church. The congregation acquired its own section of Mt. Hope Cemetery on Lemay Ferry Road in St. Louis County. At first, the Serbs allowed Russians and Romanians to be buried in their section, but voted them out in 1916.

St. Louis's Serbian community continued to strengthen through the first half of the twentieth century. The Serbian Church symbolized this cohesiveness and growth as it built a new church building in 1928 and later a social hall in 1947 at Geyer and McNair. In 1949, the congregation began welcoming large numbers of Serbian refugees to St. Louis. The church formed a committee to assist in integrating these men, women, and children into homes, employment, and schools in their new city.

Serbian refugees again poured into St. Louis in the early 1990s, and once again Holy Trinity Serbian Church extended a hand in assimilating their new community members into the fabric of St. Louis. Like the church, Serbian Americans in St. Louis embrace their American opportunities while celebrating the traditions of their homeland. The Serbian Church community invites all St. Louisans to join them in their annual SerbFest for delicious food and traditional music. How can you resist?

Hungarian

Hungary is a lovely country with lush green fields and some of the most historic buildings in the world. Those features have remained steady while the nation itself, built upon centuries of rich traditions, has endured fluctuating borders, monarchies, dictators, and occupations. Political and economic shifts have sent Hungarian immigrants streaming into the United States, many to St. Louis, for a fresh start.

The first sizable group of Hungarian immigrants found their way to St. Louis following the failed Revolution of 1848. Leaders of the so-called Hungarian War of Independence included members of the middle and upper classes. After the revolution was suppressed, many of those well-educated patriots fled the country. This migration of refugees was called the Kossuth emigration after Lajos "Louis" Kossuth, a Hungarian revolutionary. Kossuth Avenue in north St. Louis is named for the freedom fighter, and a statue of him currently sits in Fairground Park.

Born and raised in Hungary, Joseph Pulitzer immigrated to America and fought for the Union during the Civil War. He arrived in St. Louis in 1865, poor and speaking no English. Pulitzer soon became part owner of the German newspaper *Westliche Post* and served as Missouri House representative of the Fifth District of St. Louis. He purchased the *St. Louis Post-Dispatch* in 1878, taking the paper to new heights. Pulitzer later moved to New York, where he served as a congressman, ran the *World* newspaper,

and became a household name. His legacy as a journalist, politician, and philanthropist is only part of his contribution to the Mound City as a Hungarian St. Louisan.

Many Hungarians immigrated to St. Louis from the 1880s through the turn of the century, leaving the disjointed rule of the Austro-Hungarian Empire, and joining the wave of southeastern European migration. St. Louis gained Hungarian citizens of a variety of heritages, including Magyars (ethnic Hungarians), Hungarian Jews, Hungarian Slovenes, Hungarian Germans, and others.

In spite of the influx, there were too few Hungarians in St. Louis to start a Hungarian church. Unlike other cohesive immigrant communities, they settled in neighborhoods scattered around St. Louis. By the turn of the century, many Hungarians attended Holy Trinity Parish, a mostly German church on North 14th Street, which offered a Hungarian Mass. Finally, in 1934, the Reverend John Gyarmathy from Hungary founded St. Stephen of Hungary Parish at 1041 Chouteau Avenue.

In 1956, destabilization in the Hungarian homeland again triggered a wave of immigration to St. Louis. Hungarians rebelled against the Soviets, who had occupied Hungary since World War II. The Soviets brutally crushed this quest for independence dubbed "the Hungarian uprising," causing as many as two hundred thousand to flee. With the surge of new immigrants to St. Louis, the Hungarian congregation moved in 1957 from St. Steven Church to St. Mary of Victories Catholic Church, located at 3rd and Gratiot Streets in the Chouteau's Landing district of St. Louis. This lovely church had been built in 1843 for the city's German population.

Though the church continues to welcome parishioners of every ethnicity, St. Mary of Victories is home to St. Louis's Hungarian community, offering Sunday Mass in both English and Hungarian. The church serves as a community center, hosting such occasions as the Annual Hungarian Picnic and the more somber "Remembering the 1956 Hungarian Revolution" event at the church.

St. Louis's esteemed institutions of higher education play a role in serving the Hungarian community. Washington University's Clifford Holekamp offers the Danube Venture Consulting Program course, in which business students travel to Hungary to work with start-up companies. University of Missouri–St. Louis associate professor and Hungarian American Rita Csapó-Sweet was honored with the University of Missouri President's Award for Cross-Cultural Engagement for establishing institutional links with eastern European universities, including the University of Debrecen in Hungary. And the former chairman of the Saint Louis University Board of Trustees, J. Joe Adorjan, received Hungary's highest honor, the Hungarian Order of Merit–Knight's Cross, for founding

the Hungarian-Missouri Educational Partnership. The organization links four Missouri universities with five in Hungary. The program's mission is to provide scholarships for students seeking advanced degrees.

Of course, one need not receive Hungary's highest honor to serve St. Louis's Hungarian community. The Hungarian Cultural Society of St. Louis was formed to "revitalize and reignite Hungarian culture in and around the St. Louis area." The group works to foster personal, business, and educational relationships between Hungary and St. Louis. With Hungarian pastries offered by the ladies of St. Mary of Victories Church and the opportunity to learn the Hungarian language through the Hungarian Cultural Society, St. Louis is a great place to be part of the Hungarian American community.

Lebanese and Syrian

The great Ottoman Empire's history included a long rule and a long reach. In 1864, Ottoman law declared a standard provincial administration throughout the entire empire. At that time, the Ottoman's territory of Greater Syria included modern Syria, Lebanon, and a large swath of neighboring nations. St. Louis received its first immigrants from this region in the mid-nineteenth century. Between 1890 and World War I they came in droves.

At first, immigrant officials and census takers labeled the newcomers as "Asian." Later, the immigrants were documented as "Arab." In the vernacular on the streets of early twentieth-century St. Louis, all were labeled "Syrians," regardless of their ethnic heritage as Syrian, Lebanese, Turk, or others.

Some of the earliest arrivals came from the Hadchit village in the northern mountains of the Lebanese region. In St. Louis, they piled into tenement houses along the riverfront. By 1910, enough had arrived to form a tightly knit enclave in the near south side area of St. Louis called "Little Syria." Loosely bordered by Papin Street and Lafayette on the north and south, and 4th Street and 14th Street on the east and west, many of these new immigrants of Little Syria were poor and unskilled. Though they eventually developed a small group of businesses on Chouteau Avenue, they were more widely known as peddlers. These sturdy émigrés made their homes amid St. Louisans who spoke differently, dressed differently, and largely didn't like them.

As the media sometimes does, the *St. Louis Post-Dispatch* fueled adverse public opinion by its unrestrained commentary. In a 1901 article entitled "Most Undesirable Immigration," the newspaper provided data on the influx of immigrants. Citing Syrians specifically, the newspaper suggested that with the increasing numbers came "the decline of race character . . . that is, we are getting not only the bad, but the worst of the bad." In 1909, a progressive woman complained in a letter to the *Post-Dispatch* that "Turk, Syrian and other Asiatic" men are able to "escape" their class by becoming naturalized citizens, giving them the rights still withheld from American women. Such negative press continued for another decade.

But St. Louis offered the new immigrants the chance to identify with their ethnic culture. In 1898 these ethnic Lebanese immigrants established the Maronite Church of St. Anthony of the Desert. ("Maronite" refers to Christians who fled persecution into the mountains of Lebanon, where they guarded their Catholic faith.) A second Lebanese church, the Church of St. Raymond of Antioch, was founded in 1912. This house of worship became the church home for the Lebanese community of St. Louis for the next one hundred years.

As the Lebanese community worked, played, and raised families, they assimilated into the fabric of the city. But the church remained the foundation of their cultural heritage. Beginning in the mid-1970s, the St. Raymond's community welcomed new refugees fleeing the unrest of the Lebanese civil war. In 1975, a

new St. Raymond's Church building was dedicated on LaSalle Street. The building anchored a revitalization of the LaSalle Park neighborhood. For that reason, LaSalle was renamed Lebanon Drive from 11th to 7th Streets.

Today the church still stands as the cultural home for the Lebanese American community of St. Louis. The parishioners raise money for Lebanese and Syrian refugees, whose homelands still struggle with conflict. And St. Raymond's hosts its annual Lebanese festival. Where else can you enjoy live music, let the kids play, try a hookah booth, and eat your fill of foods with names like *kafta* and *kibbi nayee*? Delicious Lebanese falafel is just one of the things that makes St. Louis great.

Greek

Among the first Greek immigrants to arrive in St. Louis was George Meletio in 1868—he was in the fish business. Another was Demetrius Jannopoulo in 1871—he was in the tent and awning business. The majority of the Greeks who followed these early settlers to St. Louis came for work on the railroads. Around 1910, some Greeks from Turkey also found their way to St. Louis, seeking refuge from conflict and Turkish army conscription. It wasn't until around 1915 that Greek women and families joined these men.

The Greek immigrants established homes near each other, and their community emerged in the location of today's Busch Stadium. Greek cafes and grocery stores sprang up, supporting the families with the familiarity of home. And, like most immigrant groups, their community revolved around their church.

The St. Louis Greeks first worshipped at Holy Trinity, located at 19th and Morgan (now Delmar). The congregation, begun in 1904, struggled with a lack of cohesiveness. Yet the Greek community rallied and

in 1917 built St. Nicholas Church on Garrison Street and St. Louis Avenue. In 1918, the church opened a Greek school. The church thrived until the building was destroyed by a tornado in 1927. Undeterred, the Greek parish built themselves a beautiful new church on Forest Park Boulevard, where St. Nicholas proudly stands today.

During the 1940s, some members of the St. Louis Greek community worshipped at Assumption Greek Orthodox Church on North Euclid Avenue. The church membership grew, and the church moved first to Academy Avenue, then to Delmar Boulevard. After a fire destroyed the building in University City, the parish built the beautiful church on Des Peres Road in Town and Country, which still serves parishioners today.

The Greek American community in St. Louis immersed themselves in American culture soon after immigrating, and they established societies to ease their transition. The Hellenic American Progressive League was founded in 1919 by a group of young bachelors. Likewise, the Greek women establishedthe American Hellenic Education Progressive Association in 1920. These two charitable organizations served as the foundation for many more, which have enhanced the lives of all St. Louisans, not just the Greek Americans.

St. Louisans can worship at any of the beautiful Greek churches. Or, one might wish to attend Greek school to learn the language or the Greek style of dance. It is highly recommended, though, that one shows up at one of St. Louis's Greek festivals for music, dancing, and a delicious gyro. *Opa!*

Chinese

The first recorded Chinese immigrant arrived in St. Louis in 1857. By the 1870s, several hundred Chinese had immigrated to St. Louis. Most were men who had left their families behind, and came to St. Louis seeking factory and mine work after opportunities failed in San Francisco. In St. Louis, they stayed in boarding houses along 7th, 8th, Market, and Walnut Streets, and this section of town became known as "Hop Alley," synonymous with Chinatown.

Most did not make enough money to go back to China, and many brought their families to St. Louis instead. Making a home of Hop Alley was a hard-won triumph, as they had immigrated despite the Chinese Exclusion Act of 1882. That legislation allowed professionals to enter the United States but banned Chinese laborers. The working-class immigrants and their families were often detained until they could prove, truthfully or not, that they were of the skilled class of workers.

These Chinese immigrants started support businesses for their Hop Alley community, such as restaurants, food and herb markets, stores, and laundries. The Chinese hand laundries, however, attracted clientele outside Hop Alley. The owners subsisted frugally, often living in the backs of their laundry businesses to keep their expenses, and therefore their prices, low. Author Huping Ling described the disproportionate contribution of the St. Louis Chinese: "less than 0.1 percent of the total general population provided 60 percent of the laundry services for the city."

Like most Chinatowns, Hop Alley was viewed by St. Louisans as seedy and mysterious. But the community was cohesive and enterprising, energetic and resourceful. Safe from discrimination within their boundaries, the Hop Alley enclave was so self-sufficient that they created the On Leong Merchants and Laborers Association. Simply called On Leong, the organization was an unofficial governing body for the neighborhood.

Hop Alley remained a thriving community through the first half of the twentieth century. Then, postwar prosperity propelled parts of St. Louis, like other American cities, into urban renewal projects. In 1966, the city razed Hop Alley to make a parking lot for Busch Stadium.

From the 1960s onward, the Chinese American commercial specialty transitioned from hand laundries to restaurants and markets. Following the postwar repeal of the Chinese Exclusion Act, world-class St. Louis corporations, universities, law firms, and hospitals tapped into the reservoir of Chinese American professionals. William Tao, a Chinese American engineering graduate of Washington University, created his company William Tao and Associates in 1957. By the turn of the century, Tao's distinguished firm had helped build more than half of the structures in the St. Louis skyline.

Chinese Americans moved to different parts of the city and into the suburbs. This enterprising ethnic group

then built an alternative to the physical boundaries of Hop Alley. They constructed a "cultural community" of Chinese-language newspapers, Chinese religious institutions, and Chinese schools in which students learn language, culture, and arts. Webster University opened the door for St. Louisans of all ethnicities to learn the Chinese language and culture. The Confucius Institute, launched in 2009, is located in the historic Old Post Office building in downtown St. Louis. There, kids and adults can learn the Chinese language and participate in Chinese cultural events. Adventuresome St. Louisans can go global through the summertime opportunities to study in China.

Today, Chinese Cultural Days draws upward of ten thousand annually to the Missouri Botanical Garden. St. Louis boasts hundreds of Chinese restaurants. The Chinese American community is large, vibrant, and an important part of St. Louis.

Russian

Historians have documented a small number of Russians living in north St. Louis near the Mississippi River around 1850. More Russians immigrated to St. Louis toward the turn of the century. At that time in Russia, Alexander III ruled with a heavy hand, "Russianizing" its citizens. One of his policies determined that every Russian speak only the Russian language, in spite of the varying ethnic groups within the empire. Additionally, St. Louis became a refuge for Russian Jews fleeing persecution.

Some of these new immigrants moved into Kerry Patch, the haven in northwest St. Louis for Irish immigrants. The 1910 census revealed that over thirteen thousand St. Louisans were Russian immigrants, many of them Jews. Not all, however. St. Michael the Archangel Church was established in 1909. The church's parishioners comprised immigrants from eastern Europe and Russia. Their first house of worship was a converted home on Hickory Street. Then, in 1929, their beautiful church was built at Ann Avenue and Gravois, where it continues to serve ethnic Russians as well as other ethnicities today.

Russian immigration continued sporadically throughout the twentieth century. The 1930 census indicated a large Russian population in University City, still home to many ethnic Russians. Russian Americans also worship at St. John Chrysostom Orthodox Church, founded in 1983 in House Springs, Missouri, on the outskirts of St. Louis. St. Basil the Great Orthodox Church on McCausland provides another religious center for Russian Americans in

St. Louis. The Russian-American School of St. Louis teaches the Russian language to children and adults, preserving the language and culture of Russia and enhancing diversity in St. Louis.

St. Louis's sister city relationship with Samara, Russia, began in 1992 with the prompting of educators from Southern Illinois University Edwardsville and Webster University who taught English at Samara State University. The Greater St. Louis–Samara Sister Cities Committee is an all-volunteer organization that "represents Greater St. Louis in all ongoing cultural exchange and economic development with the Russian sister city." The committee works with hospitals, universities, and regional municipalities and businesses to further promote St. Louis's ties to Russia.

Bulgarian

Bulgaria was part of the Ottoman Empire for five hundred years. Though the tiny Slavic nation gained its independence during the Russo-Turkish War of 1877–1878, the Turks continued their attempts to subjugate the Macedonian Bulgarians. Many fled and found their long, long way to the Illinois side of metropolitan St. Louis. Back in Bulgaria, the nation's people attempted an uprising in 1903. The Ilinden Uprising was suppressed, resulting in the largest mass migration out of Macedonia.

In the 1890s, the Niedringhaus brothers, barons of St. Louis industry in granite and steel, purchased four thousand acres of land just across the Mississippi River in Illinois. Economically, the inexpensive land and river access provided sound reasons to build their enterprises across the river, while maintaining their offices a mere stone's throw away in St. Louis. The Niedringhauses incorporated the town of Granite City, which, along with the nearby towns of Madison and Venice, soon became a major industrial center. The massive influx of immigrating Bulgarians filled the need for unskilled labor.

Most of the Bulgarians who settled in the tri-city area were male. In fact, writes Bulgarian immigration scholar David Cassens, "Among the eight thousand to ten thousand Bulgarians living in the tri-cities in 1905, there were only four families." These men lived in bachelor housing called the *boort*—overcrowded and dirty lodging houses in a section of Granite City dubbed "Hungry Hollow." This area remained primarily male until World War I.

The Bulgarian community produced six newspapers. The most significant, *Naroden Glas* (People's Voice), owned its own printing press and operated the largest Bulgarian bookstore in North America. Following the devastating economic depression of 1907–1908, the Bulgarians rallied. Symbolizing their stability as a thriving community, the immigrants planned the building of their first church. In 1909, Saints Cyril and Methodius in Granite City became the first Bulgarian Orthodox church in North America. The following year, a second Bulgarian Orthodox church—Holy Trinity—was erected in Madison.

In 1919, Holy Trinity burned to the ground. Nearly a decade later, the community rebuilt the church on the same location. Saints Cyril and Methodius Church was sold to the Armenian congregation in the 1930s, and Holy Trinity has served the entire metro St. Louis region since. The parish enlarged the church building in 1974–1975, adding breathtaking religious icons.

St. Louis welcomed more Bulgarian immigrants in the 1990s as the country struggled to shed its post–World War II Soviet communist influence. Though not as numerous or cohesive as those of the early 1900s, the Bulgarians of St. Louis commemorate their ethnic origins. The Bulgarian Spirit is a dance corps comprising Bulgarians from the St. Louis community. Sharing their love of Bulgarian culture, the group dances in events such as the hugely popular Festival of Nations in Tower Grove Park. Through dance, the group celebrates the spirit of Bulgarians in St. Louis, whose way was paved by the Bulgarians of Hungry Hollow.

Czech

Bohemia was part of the Ottoman Empire in 1848, when its Czech citizens began a steady flow of immigration to St. Louis. They fled the oppression of the Hapsburg dynasty, turning instead to the political and religious freedoms of Middle America. Most Czechs spoke German, which allowed them to easily integrate with the multitudes of Germans immigrating to St. Louis at the same time.

The first to arrive settled on what quickly became known as Bohemian Hill in south St. Louis, around 9th Street and Lafayette Avenue. In 1890, nearly eight thousand Czechs called St. Louis home, many of whom lived on Bohemian Hill. By the turn of the century, the neighborhood was surrounded by Park, Allen, Broadway, and 18th Street. These industrious newcomers worked in breweries, mills, factories, and mines.

Although Catholics and Protestants were sharply divided in Bohemia, Czechs of both faiths lived peacefully in St. Louis, along with a few Bohemian Jews. In 1854, Father Henry Lipovsky led the construction of a Catholic church on the corner of 11th and Soulard Streets. By the end of the nineteenth century, the Czech congregation of St. John Nepomuk included a membership of immigrants from other southeastern European nations. St. John's also built a Czech Catholic school in 1869. Between 1860 and 1890, the Czech population in St. Louis tripled. St. Wenceslaus, a second Czech Catholic church and school, was built in 1894 on Bohemian Hill at 3014 Oregon Avenue.

Several contributing factors led to the demise of Bohemian Hill. Following World War I, Czechoslovakia declared its independence from the Austro-Hungarian Empire, so Czechs no longer fled the Hapsburg oppression. This, coupled with restrictive American immigration laws, slowed Czech immigration to St. Louis. Then, in the 1920s and 1930s, many second-generation residents of Bohemian Hill found homes elsewhere in St. Louis. More than half of the historic homes in Bohemian Hill were destroyed in the 1950s to make way for public housing. Around that time, the Czech newspaper *Hlas* went out of print after serving the St. Louis Czech community for nearly one hundred years, delivering a final blow to the once-thriving Bohemian Hill community.

Despite the end of Bohemian Hill, several structures near the St. John's buildings near 12th Street and Lafayette were recognized for their historic significance. They were placed on the National Register of Historic Places as the St. John Nepomuk Parish Historic District in the 1970s. This was one of numerous revitalization efforts that contributed to the beauty and charm of today's Soulard area.

The thriving American Czech Educational Center in south St. Louis continues to serve as a social center for Czechs and Slovaks of the St. Louis region. This association derived from the Czecho-Slovak Protective Society and the Sokol, both Czech organizations founded in the mid-nineteenth century. These institutions have lasted a century and a half and have stood the test of time, while the borders of the Czech homeland evolved: in 1993, the former Czechoslovakia divided into the Czech Republic and Slovakia. The longevity of this important organization stands as a tribute to the wherewithal of the St. Louis Czech community, from the heyday of Bohemian Hill until today.

Slovak

Men and women of Slovak descent in St. Louis carry with them a storied history of their ancestors. Some of the earliest ethnic Slovaks made their way to St. Louis following the failed Revolution of 1848, an uprising that spread nationalistic fervor across Europe and throughout the Habsburg dynasty. More immigrated as the century progressed, disillusioned by the lack of representation within the Austro-Hungarian Empire. By the turn of the century, a large number of Slovak immigrants settled with the Czechs on Bohemian Hill.

Newly arrived Catholic Slovaks joined the Czech congregation of St. John Nepomuk, which first built its church at 11th and Soulard Streets in 1854, then in Bohemian Hill on Oregon Avenue in 1894. A few years later, the Slovak Catholics began their own parish. They purchased a former Baptist church at 1145 Park Avenue and dedicated their new house of worship, Most Holy Trinity, in 1898. In the 1920s, the congregation swelled to five hundred families. The parish moved into a former Evangelical church near

9th and Soulard in 1924, forced to relocate as the city of St. Louis widened 12th Boulevard.

Lutheran Slovak immigrants founded their own church, Slovak Evangelical Lutheran Church, in 1905. The group met at "Old Trinity," a church at South 8th and Soulard. In 1909, the congregation worshipped in a three-story building they purchased at 1921 South 9th Street. A few years later, they moved into a proper church building at 13th Street and Allen Avenue. The congregation moved for the last time into a church they built at Morganford Road and Blow Street, dedicated in 1958.

Members of both congregations no doubt joined the greater St. Louis Slovak community in celebrating the official formation of Czecho-Slovakia in 1918, a triumph of World War I. The *St. Louis Post-Dispatch* reported on the celebration. Thousands of St. Louisans of all ethnicities lined the streets as the Jefferson Barracks Band led a parade from Bohemian Hall at 9th and Allen to city hall. Speeches were given in Czech, Slovak, and English by dignitaries Missouri lieutenant governor Wallace Crossley, St. Louis mayor Henry Kiel, and Archbishop John J. Glennon. The new flag of the infant nation was flown over St. Louis City Hall. St. Louis embraced the momentous occasion as the immigrants celebrated both their new nation and their new homeland.

In many ways, the Slovak community in St. Louis today carries on the traditions of the early Slovak immigrants. The American Czech Educational

Center at 4690 Lansdowne Avenue, home of Sokol St. Louis, offers gymnastics classes and exhibitions. Czech and Slovak immigrants founded the Sokol in south St. Louis, the first in the United States, in 1854. The Sokol (a Czech and Slovak society) provided gymnastic exercise and social activities, just as it does today.

The Slovak Republic became an independent nation in 1993. St. Louis showed less fanfare at this milestone of its Slovak citizenry, but the contributions of Slovak St. Louisans are recognized. Such Slovak hockey greats as Pavol Demitra, Jaroslav Halak, Michal Handzus, and Vladimir Orszagh have skated their way into the hearts of St. Louis Blues fans.

Holy Trinity, the first Slovak church, closed its doors in 1982, but St. Lucas lives on. The church now serves St. Louisans from all walks of life and continues to stay grounded in its Slovak traditions. Their annual Slovak Festival is one of their greatest contributions to the St. Louis region. The Slovak language was last preached in its worship services as recently as 1985. Regarding this, the church represents the philosophy of St. Louis: "As the community changes, so does the spiritual service adapt to its new and future family representing a diversity of backgrounds." Well said.

Croatian

When Croatian immigrants arrived in St. Louis in the 1860s, they formed a colony downtown near 2nd and Market Streets. The first arrivals would have had no way of knowing that they were planting seeds for a vibrant community that, over the course of the next century and a half, would become a vital and dynamic collective that would maintain close ties and fierce attachments to the Croatian homeland. The first Croatians were likely secondary migrants from the lower Mississippi River areas near Louisiana, who had originally come from the southern Dalmatian region of Croatia. Experienced seamen, these first arrivals brought with them advanced nautical skills and extensive knowledge of fishing that had been passed down through generations in the towns and islands of the southern Adriatic.

Like later immigrants, the first Croatians to arrive in St. Louis brought with them the lived experience and collective memory of what it meant to be a Croat, members of a South Slavic ethnic group in south central Europe on the eastern Adriatic who lived mainly in Croatia (then part of the Austro-Hungarian Empire) and in neighboring Bosnia-Herzegovina, where Roman Catholics considered themselves to be part of the Croatian people.

From the beginning, Croatians in St. Louis formed mutual benefit associations. Already in 1893, a group was established called the Croatian-Slovenian Roman Catholic Benevolent Society of Saints Cyril and Methodius. Later, other religious societies were organized, such as Sv. Nikola, Sveto Srce Marijevo,

and the Croatian Catholic Union. Croatian singing societies were formed, such as Sloboda and Vila. Sokols, similar to the German turner halls popular in St. Louis at the time, were established, including Hrvatski Sokol and Sokol Dalmacija. Croatian Fraternal Society Lodges 49 and 50 continue to meet at St. Joseph's Croatian Church.

Despite transition, dispersion, and crisis, St. Joseph's Croatian Catholic Church in Soulard has remained a fixture of continuity and stability and has played a central role in the creation and maintenance of a distinctly Croatian identity among generations of St. Louisans of Croatian heritage. In 1904, the same year as the World's Fair in St. Louis, Catholic Croatians organized themselves around their common faith and asked St. Louis archbishop John J. Glennon for permission to start a Croatian-language church.

Initially housed in a vacant Jewish synagogue purchased at 11th and Chouteau, the Croatian Church quickly outgrew its quarters there and established St. Joseph's Parish at its present location at 12th and Russell in Soulard. The Croatian Church had a grade school, where the Croatian language was taught. By the 1950s, with the decline of Croatians living close to the parish, the school was closed.

Nevertheless, the Croatian community maintained ties to St. Joseph's Church, with many returning each Sunday for Mass in Croatian. As waves of new arrivals came to St. Louis, their first stop was St. Joseph's Church. Sometimes arriving with suitcases still in hand, they received information about immigration papers, jobs, housing, transportation, and other practical daily needs in navigating the new culture, such as how to see doctors and deal with traffic tickets.

Additionally, Croatians socialize in various groups associated with the Croatian Church, where they have picnics and parties, listen to Croatian music, and roast lamb. Many children who are members of the parish take folklore lessons of *tamburitza* playing and *kolo* dancing, as well as Croatian singing.

The revival of interest in events at home among Croatians living in St. Louis was extremely intense during the wars of dissolution in the former Yugoslavia in the early 1990s. The Croatian community mobilized with the creation of the American Croatian Relief Project (ACRP), which organized major relief efforts to deliver humanitarian aid supplies to refugees and displaced persons. Action and advocacy on behalf of Croatia was accompanied by a revival of national pride, marked by renewed interest in the study of the Croatian language. Croatian language classes that have been offered in St. Louis for more than thirty years, taught by Nasja Bošković Meyer, a native of Split, found an even wider and receptive audience. The influx of Bosnian refugees in St. Louis made even more Americans become interested in the Croatian language, which is similar to Bosnian.

Polish

Poland disappeared from the map in 1795, when it was partitioned by the Kingdom of Prussia, the Russian Empire, and the Austrian Habsburg monarchy. Nearly a century later, the first Poles made their way to St. Louis. In the 1870s they fled Bismarck's efforts to Germanize the Polish section of Prussia, the Russian conscription, and anti-Catholic policies.

During the 1860s and 1870s, Poles in St. Louis made up less than 1 percent of the population. The largest group of Poles lived in St. Louis's near north side, from Biddle to Franklin, and on Carr, Morgan, and O'Fallon Streets. During the last two decades of the nineteenth century, the number of Polish immigrants increased substantially, lured by industry in St. Louis.

The St. Louis Polish community, or Polonia, never established a cohesive geographic pocket of the city. They scattered into different neighborhoods, from the German south side to the Irish Kerry Patch. However, most lived on the near north side or at the river's edge, where the new Eads Bridge and the river trade often brought the most promise of employment. Regardless of where the Poles lived, they found themselves in the most impoverished neighborhoods in the city. Facing heavy discrimination, many Poles lived in crime-ridden slums.

Yet they persevered. Like most ethnic groups, the St. Louis Polish community was centered around their faith. Polish Catholics attended Mass with the Irish and Germans until they established their first church, St. Stanislaus Kostka. The house of worship was built in 1880 on the west side of 20th Street, south of Cass Avenue. To meet the needs of their growing membership, they built a new church a decade later. By 1900, around 2,300 people attended weekly services and 450 children attended the church's school. The church's benevolent societies included the Franciscan Sisters of Our Lady of Perpetual Help, whose mission was to educate poor children of Polish immigrants.

Another Roman Catholic church and school, St. Casimir, was established in 1889 at 8th and Mound. This parish had formed out of St. Stanislaus Kostka Church. In 1895, they built themselves a new church at 8th and Mullanphy. By 1912, some 650 families attended St. Casimir and 700 children were enrolled in the school.

The St. Louis Polonia established two other Roman Catholic churches: St. Hedwig in 1904 and Our Lady of Czestochowa in 1907. St. Hedwig built first at Itaska and Compton, then moved to 3202 Pulaski. Our Lady of Czestochowa moved into a building at 4th and Victor. Additionally, the Polish National Catholic Church (independent of the Roman Catholic Church) established Saints Cyril and Methodius Parish in 1907 at North 11th and Chambers Streets.

From the lengthy list of churches that served the St. Louis Polish community, it is evident that the Poles' faith played an important role in their new lives in America. As the Polish American community assimilated and the city's physical footprint changed, several of these churches closed their doors. In 1957, the St. Casimir Church building was demolished to

make way for Interstate 70. The parish relocated to Vorhof and Ainsworth Drives, then closed for good in 1992. Our Lady of Czestochowa closed in 1957, and St. Hedwig School closed in 1970 and its parish in 2005. St. Stanislaus Kostka, the "mother church" of the other three former Roman Catholic churches in St. Louis, became engaged in a disagreement with the Roman Catholic Church in 2005, making national news. The church, now no longer part of the Roman Catholic Church, continues to serve St. Louisans, even offering a weekly Mass in Polish.

Today, beautiful weddings are held on North 20th Street at the Polish Heritage Center. Children attend a Polish church school at St. Agatha Church on South 9th Street. And the Polish community thrives in other ways: St. Louisans can tune into a polka radio station, watch *TV Cracovia*, or attend functions held by the St. Louis Polonia and the Polish American Cultural Society of Metro St. Louis. The Polonia of St. Louis began in difficult circumstances, but they endured. Their industrious nature, their national pride, and their lively polka music are an important piece of St. Louis today.

Romanian

The first known Romanian immigrant to St. Louis, Ion Croitoru, received his citizenship papers in 1898. He and those who followed, most arriving before World War II, settled largely in south St. Louis neighborhoods. Many of these Romanian newcomers attended the Albanian or Greek churches until their own church was built. St. Thomas the Apostle Church, established in 1935, developed out of Romanian and Macedo-Romanian fraternal societies in St. Louis. The parish was first located on Missouri Avenue, then relocated to Compton Avenue in 1954. In 1959, the Romanian American community built their lovely church at its current location on Nottingham Avenue. For a taste of St. Louis Romanian ethnicity, enjoy a festival at historic St. Thomas the Apostle or sample some Romanian food at the new Holy Trinity Romanian Church of God on Marmaduke.

Dutch

Unlike many ethnic groups, the Dutch did not immigrate to St. Louis in large population waves. Many Netherlanders opted for farmland in the Upper Midwest, and some stayed in St. Louis after visiting en route. Sadly, an example of this is in 1848. Immigrants from Germany and Holland fled the cholera epidemic in their homelands. They struck out for America and were quarantined after transferring the sickness to the cities of New Orleans and St. Louis. Those who survived, stayed.

Dutch Jews found a home in St. Louis among the large Jewish population. St. Louis was also a Catholic center, and the Catholic immigrants from Holland readily worshipped with those from Germany, Belgium, and Ireland. There were not enough Catholics from the Netherlands in St. Louis to form a parish with a Dutch-speaking priest. There were, though, enough Dutch in St. Louis for the Kingdom of the Netherlands to appoint a consul in St. Louis in 1851. Except for brief transition periods, there has been a consul of the Netherlands in St. Louis ever since.

In early 1978, a handful of Dutch Americans gauged the interest in forming a Dutch club. Over 75 people responded, and the Netherlands Society of St. Louis has been active since. As a social club for those of Dutch descent or those interested in the cultural heritage of Holland, the group holds annual events such as picnics in the summer and a Sinterklaas

(St. Nicholas) celebration in December. The society shares ethnic Dutch meals, wears orange (the national color) in support of Dutch sports teams competing internationally, and welcomes new Dutch immigrants.

Norwegian

Few Norwegians immigrated to St. Louis, preferring instead the farming communities of the northern plains and the Upper Midwest. Despite this, census records indicate a small number of Norwegian families lived in St. Louis from 1880 to 1930. Today, though, the Norwegian Society of St. Louis is dedicated to promoting the heritage of Norwegian Americans living in the greater St. Louis area. They achieve this through events, language classes, and the annual Scandinavian picnic with their Danish and Swedish friends.

Swedish

There were so many Swedish immigrants in St. Louis by 1889 that the new settlers established the Swedish National Society. The society was created to ease the transition of new immigrants from Sweden. Most Swedish immigrants in St. Louis settled in the Rock Springs neighborhood, near today's Saint Louis University High School. The community stretched from Sarah to Vandeventer, north of Manchester. The Swedes immersed themselves into American life; many worked at a nearby shovel factory. The Swedish community's band marched in the opening parade of the 1904 World's Fair.

The Swedes established Gethsemane Lutheran Church in 1894. The congregation met in rented halls until 1899, when they built their first chapel at California and Rutger Streets. That year, the membership included sixty-seven adults and forty-three children, and all of the services were held in

Swedish. To promote assimilation, the church began offering one service in English on one evening per month in 1900.

The congregation grew as more Swedish immigrants arrived in St. Louis. In 1909, the church purchased a church building on St. Vincent. The membership proudly added a pipe organ six years later. By 1924, all services were held in English. Meanwhile, the Swedish National Society's membership had grown so much that, in 1913, the group built a building at 1157 South Kingshighway. The society thrived for many years, but by the 1960s fell victim to membership struggles as a result of diminished Swedish immigration and assimilation. The society disbanded and sold its building in 1969.

Gethsemane Lutheran Church, on the other hand, grew. In 1945, its congregation elected to build a new church on Hampton Avenue. The congregation met at Mallinckrodt School to worship while the church was under construction. The congregation moved into the new building in 1948, and the church continues to serve the community at that location today.

With renewed interest in Swedish culture, the Swedish Council of St. Louis was organized in 1976. Established to promote knowledge and preservation of Swedish heritage, the group hosts numerous cultural events and provides resources for Swedish language instruction, folk dancing, and other educational programs. The Swedish Council also contributed to the restoration of the Linnean House at the Missouri Botanical Garden. The Linnean House was named for

Swedish botanist Carl Linnaeus, who, according to the garden, "laid the foundation for the modern scheme of binomial nomenclature." The Linnean House is the oldest continuously operated public greenhouse west of the Mississippi River.

The stately building on South Kingshighway, decorated with the words "Swedish National Society Building" over its imposing doorway, was torn down in 2013, erasing the last physical trace of the early Swedish immigrants. But those of Swedish heritage, with their church and their council, keep the knowledge of Swedish heritage alive in St. Louis today.

Danish

Bethany Lutheran Church, on Fairview Avenue in Webster Groves, is a standing testament to early Danish settlers in the St. Louis area. These immigrants, who arrived in the late nineteenth century, constructed the church in 1904. At that time, a Danish artist who was working at the World's Fair painted the scene on the church's altar. Well-known Dane Bonnie Rasmussen, renowned for her woodcarvings and daughter of one of the church's founders, crafted the Viking ship that hangs in the front of the sanctuary. Fellow Danes continue to worship in and beautify the church.

While Danish immigrants are not, nor have ever been, the largest immigrant group in St. Louis, their contributions remain today. The House of Denmark, a contemporary furniture store with locations on Olive Boulevard and Tesson Ferry Road, has been owned and operated by Danes since its opening in 1977. And the ever-active Danish Club of St. Louis shares news from Denmark, offers Danish recipes, has social gatherings, and bids *Velkommen*! to all who wish to join.

A CITY ON DISPLAY TO THE WORLD: 1904

By the time of the 1904 World's Fair, immigrants of the mid-nineteenth century had firmly established themselves as the backbone of the city. The contributions of foreign-born citizens and their American-born children made St. Louis an example of a successful city for immigrants. Nevertheless, the prospect of putting on an exposition was a massive undertaking. The city cleaned its coal-filled air, electrified its homes, paved its streets, and filtered its water by the time the world descended on Forest Park for the World's Fair.

CONTRACTION AND CHANGE: 1940 TO 1980s

As the century progressed, immigrants who had arrived in the late nineteenth century found their footing. They established houses of worship and community enclaves, and by 1940 over 800,000 people lived in the city of St. Louis.

After World War II, the city welcomed war refugees, but St. Louis's population peaked at 856,000 by 1950. Migration to the suburbs and marriages outside ethnic groups diffused individual ethnic identities. St. Louis settled into a period of quiet stability.

Immigrant laws changed in the mid-1960s, and the face of St. Louis once again grew in diversity with an influx of Asian immigrants. These newcomers brought with them more foreign languages, customs, and foods, permanently enriching the landscape of St. Louis. While some ethnic houses of worship closed their doors in the city, more mosques, churches, and temples sprang up in the suburbs, spreading the ethnic diversification of the city into the surrounding St. Louis region.

NEW ARRIVALS: A HOME FAR FROM HOME—1980s TO THE PRESENT

Just as it had in the late nineteenth century, St. Louis became a beacon for refugees in the 1980s and the 1990s—a phenomenon that continues today. Men, women, and children from war-torn nations find a haven in St. Louis. Like new immigrants one hundred years before them, they encounter in St. Louis a completely new culture. With the help of already established immigrant groups, religious organizations, and the International Institute, foreign-born newcomers settle in St. Louis for a new beginning. St. Louis, as a result, continues its tradition as a vibrant, multiethnic city, boasting foods and festivals that celebrate its citizens from around the world. St. Louis is a place not just to start anew, but to stay.

ASIA

Bhutanese
Taiwanese
Korean
Nepalese
Indian Bangladeshi
Japanese
Sri Lankan

ASIA

Bangladeshi

St. Louis has an active Bangladeshi community. In 1985, members of the community established the Bangladesh Association of Greater St. Louis. This nonprofit organization seeks to "promote Bangladeshi culture and heritage to the young Bangladesh-Americans as well as to the people of other countries and cultures."

While most Bangladeshi practice Islam, people from that nation also worship as Hindus, Buddhists, Christians, and others. In making their home in St. Louis, Bangladeshi newcomers integrate the old with the new, working to uphold their association's mission, "To develop and promote friendly relationships among the members of the community and with other people in the metropolitan area of Greater St. Louis."

Bhutanese

Bhutan is a tiny country. Politically and economically isolated, it is landlocked between India and China. Cultural and religious differences led to unrest, and many fled to Nepal for refuge. In 2008, St. Louis welcomed those refugees arriving in America seeking a fresh start.

The International Institute, St. Louis's welcome mat for refugees, has aided the newcomers in their resettlement. According to the International Institute, the Bhutanese are the fourth-largest immigrant group in St. Louis.

The Bhutanese Association of St. Louis helps its people successfully conquer the challenges of language and cultural differences. The association helps bridge the gap between their Asian roots and their new St. Louis home. Some St. Louis Bhutanese practice Hinduism or Buddhism. Others are Christian, and many have found a church home at New City in south St. Louis. A haven for newly arrived immigrants from around the world, New City is an offshoot of the New City Fellowship congregation in University City, founded in 2004.

It's not just the refugees who benefit from the fresh start in St. Louis. The city is a better place for the Bhutanese men and women who have brought with them inner strength, open minds, and willing hands.

Indian

After a change in immigration laws in 1965, the door opened for Indians and people of other Asian nations to immigrate to the United States. Over the next few decades, the population of people of Indian descent in St. Louis expanded. Many of these early arrivals were well educated, and sought employment in the sciences, medicine, and engineering. Indian families faced language and cultural challenges such as style of dress and a new food palette. Tales of carpooling to Chicago to acquire foods at an Indian grocery store mark these early immigrants as true pioneers. Today, St. Louis is home to Indian restaurants and markets, which provide tasty food for St. Louis customers from all walks of life.

The Indian community of St. Louis, largely assimilated, maintains ties with those of their own heritage. The India Association of St. Louis "celebrates India's cultural heritage, educates their children about India's history, promotes better relationships among communities, and assists people in times of distress." Likewise, Bal Vihar, the Center for Indian Cultural Education, provides Indian cultural education for children to "foster and preserve Asian cultural values."

Indian immigrants brought with them the religions of their land, including Hinduism, Sikhism, Islam, and Christianity. Indian Americans of St. Louis attend temples and churches throughout the region, including the Hare Krishna Temple on Lindell Boulevard and the Sikh Temple on Willis Road in St. Peters. Dar-ul-Islam, the Mahatma Gandhi Cultural Center, and the Hindu Temple of St. Louis are all located on Weidman Road in Ballwin. The Hindu Temple is truly an architectural gem.

As in India, the St. Louis Indian community is diverse. Varying ethnic groups have retained their diversity in their new American city, as attested by the many cultural associations. They include the Telugu Association of Saint Louis, Tamil Sangam, the Sangama Kannada Association, the St. Louis Marathi Mandal, and Punascha. Sangeetha, another cultural society, promotes Indian classical music. Supported by esteemed organizations such as the Regional Arts Commission, Missouri Arts Council, and the Arts & Education Council, Sangeetha is recognized as a premier cultural society.

The Network of Indian Professionals is not just a networking forum, but aspires "to be the facilitating vehicle used by South Asian professionals to improve and enhance the communities in which we work and live." Vibrant and active Indian student associations add energy to nearly every regional university in St. Louis. Additionally, Asha–St. Louis, formed in 1996 at Washington University, is dedicated to increasing literacy among children in India.

Indian Americans living in St. Louis have not limited their contributions to professionalism, food, religion, and culture. Did you know St. Louis has a thriving cricket league? Check it out the next time the Cardinals are out of town.

Japanese

Japan's military might at the turn of the twentieth century drew the admiration of many Americans. Tourists marveled at their architecture, art, and gardens as they milled about the Japanese exhibit at the 1904 World's Fair in Forest Park. Following the fair, some Japanese remained in St. Louis, becoming permanent residents of the Gateway City. By the beginning of World War II, at least eleven Japanese families called St. Louis home.

The world grew dark during the war. The American government seized the property of Japanese Americans, forcing them to live in "relocation centers" (internment camps) between 1942 and 1945. Japanese American college students faced relocation from West Coast schools to those in the interior. Washington University chose to accept displaced students. Chancellor George Throop proclaimed, "The attitude of the University is that these students, if American citizens, have exactly the same rights as other students who desire to register in the University." Nearly thirty Japanese American students transferred to Washington University during the war, enjoying the freedoms of all students on the campus. One, Gyo Obata, finished the degree at Washington University that he had started at the University of California–Berkeley. He then joined with fellow architecture alumni to form the now world-renowned St. Louis–based architectural firm of Hellmuth, Obata & Kassabaum (HOK).

Following the disgrace of internment, approximately 350 families settled in St. Louis to make a new life after the war. During the 1950s, around 150 servicemen moved to St. Louis with their Japanese wives. As a result of their war experience, the new St. Louisans formed a chapter of the Japanese-American Citizens League in 1946. The organization was founded to promote and protect equal rights for Americans of Japanese descent, and it continues with that undertaking today.

The Japan America Society of St. Louis was founded in 1967 with the mission of promoting the exchange and understanding between the people of Japan and the United States. Several equally active organizations emerged from the society, including the Japanese Activities Committee, the Japan America Society Women's Association, and Seinen-kai (Association of Young Men and Women). The society also sponsors the Japanese Language School of St. Louis. The society boasts close relations with the International Studies and Programs and the Shibusawa-Arai Endowed Professorship of Japanese Studies at the University of Missouri–St. Louis. It also acts in partnership with the school's Japan America Student Association.

The influence of the Japanese American community extended to the Missouri Botanical Garden. In 1977,

the garden dedicated its new Seiwa-en, or Japanese Garden. At fourteen acres, the Japanese Garden is one of the largest in North America, representing "an evolution of centuries of tradition and a multiplicity of distinctly Japanese cultural influences." The Missouri Botanical Garden's largest community engagement is the Japanese Festival, which attracts approximately forty thousand visitors per year. Hosted by the Japan America Society, the Japanese Festival celebrates the history and culture of Japan, showcasing dancing, music, and martial arts.

For year-round martial arts, St. Louisans can study at Ki Aikido, a school for martial arts located on Pershing Avenue. Since 1979, the school has devoted its entire curriculum to the study of aikido, a martial art of Japanese origin; mind/body oneness; and ki aikido, centered on motivation enhanced by calmness.

St. Louisans of Japanese descent practice multiple religions, represented in the houses of worship dedicated to the Japanese American population in the city. These include the Japanese International Harvest Church on Manchester Road in Brentwood, the Center for Pragmatic Buddhism in the Central West End, the Missouri Zen Center in Webster Groves, and the Fo Guang Shan St. Louis Buddhist Center in Bridgeton.

St. Louisans of all ethnicities benefit from the sister city relationship with Suwa, Japan. Since 1974, the two cities have exchanged cultural events and have facilitated communication between countries for corporations and small businesses. Japanese businesses with U.S. operations in St. Louis include Aluman Foils, Consolidated Grain & Barge, Mitsubishi Trading, and Koken Manufacturing.

Japanese culture is showcased in the Asian Art Collection at the Saint Louis Art Museum. The collection includes Buddhist sculpture, Japanese calligraphy, painting, and folding screens. Of course, one should include in this feast for the senses a trip to one of St. Louis's many Asian markets or dinner at Nobu, located at 8643 Olive Boulevard. That's but one example from a broad spectrum of Japanese cuisine, right here in St. Louis.

Korean

Following the change in immigration legislation in 1965, Korean immigrants walked through the open doors of St. Louis for the first time in large numbers. The improved quota system was the keystone to the legislation shift, enabling the immigration of Asians to the United States, and into St. Louis. Today, Korean Americans can find hospitality through such organizations as the Korean-American Association of St. Louis, the Young Asian-American Professional Association, the Asian-American Chamber of Commerce, and the St. Louis Chapter of the Organization of Chinese Americans–Asian Pacific American Advocates.

Churches and religious organizations offering services to Korean Americans dot metro St. Louis. St. Louisans can find books in Asian languages in the extensive collections of the St. Louis County Library's Daniel Boone Branch. And a connection can be found through Anheuser-Busch InBev, a name synonymous with St. Louis. The brewery recently reacquired Oriental Brewery, formerly South Korea's largest brewer. The ethnic beer and ethnic food are just two of the reasons St. Louis embraces its citizens of Korean descent.

Nepalese

Nepal and its neighboring nations share a diverse population, comprising peoples defined by culture, ethnicity, religion, and even language. Furthering the complexity, traditional Nepalese originate from Nepal as well as historic communities of Nepali origin in southern Bhutan. Regardless of their roots, many Nepalese immigrants have made their long way to St. Louis.

So many, in fact, that the self-proclaimed "energetic group of Nepalese" founded the Greater St. Louis Nepali Chautari. The organization was established to "facilitate social togetherness through different cultural activities." The association boasts a membership of Nepalese and friends of Nepalese living in and around the greater St. Louis area.

While the immigrants represent multiple religions, many Nepalese Christians congregate at the Christian Friends of New Americans Center on South Grand. This extension of the Ascension Lutheran Church offers worship services in the Nepalese language. St. Louisans also extend their hand to Nepalese through the Mitrata Nepal Foundation for Children, a nonprofit organization dedicated to providing education, housing, and medical care for underprivileged children of Nepal. Similarly, the Himalayan Family Healthcare Project, founded by a Nepalese American St. Louisan, works to provide health care and education in remote areas of Nepal.

Meanwhile, in St. Louis, Nepalese immigrants and adventuresome St. Louisans can get a taste of Nepal at the Gurung Bazaar, the Nepali-International store at Grand and Chippewa.

Sri Lankan

Sri Lankan immigrants in St. Louis initially gathered purely on a social basis in each other's homes in the 1970s. In 1980, the Sri Lankan Association officially formed, and the group has been active since. The organization comprises Sri Lankan immigrants as well as second- and third-generation Sri Lankan Americans from St. Louis and the Midwest. The association represents various Sri Lankan regions and religions, making it "a true representation of the pluralistic Sri Lankan society."

A coup for the Sri Lankan community took place in 1983, when a member of the Sri Lankan Association was tapped as the official escort for Miss Sri Lanka, who competed in the Miss Universe Pageant in St. Louis that year. Socially and philanthropically, the Sri Lankan community is a great contributor to the ethnic diversity of St. Louis.

Taiwanese

Taiwanese immigrants came to St. Louis as early as the 1950s. Largely educated, many came to study, taking advantage of St. Louis's top-notch medical facilities and universities. The St. Louis branch of the North American Taiwanese Medical Association stands as a testament to the contributions of the Taiwanese to the city's medical community. The organization promotes the cultural and educational exchange of Taiwanese American medical, dental, and allied health professionals. By the 1980s, the majority of immigrants from Taiwan came to St. Louis looking to work in business. As workers in both medicine and commerce, the Taiwanese community continues to add energy to St. Louis.

Like most immigrant groups, the Taiwanese represent numerous faiths. The Taiwanese Presbyterian Church of Greater St. Louis has become a church home for many. The church was founded in the early 1970s by immigrants from Taiwan. Located on Ries Road in Ballwin, the congregation comprises various ethnic backgrounds, and the church offers services in both English and Mandarin.

Like the many Buddhist temples in St. Louis, the Fo Guang Shan St. Louis Buddhist Center not only welcomes Taiwanese but embraces all ethnicities and traditions. The order's objectives are to promote Humanistic Buddhism and to bring forth faith, joy, hope, and service for all. The center was founded in 1999 and made its permanent home in 2006 on Smiley Road in Bridgeton.

The St. Louis Taiwanese celebrate their common ethnicity through the Taiwanese Association of America in Greater St. Louis. Among other cultural and educational missions, the group works to preserve Taiwanese American heritage, advance the understanding of Taiwanese culture, and contribute to the diversity of St. Louis. The association's goal is to cultivate fellowship and harmony among St. Louisans. In addition to other events, the association conducts the Taiwanese American Heritage Celebration, including a free concert. Celebrating Eastern and Western music at the Sheldon Concert Hall is a great way for all St. Louisans to enjoy the blending of cultures.

SOUTHEAST ASIA

Philippines

Singapore

Malaysia

East Timor

Thailand

Laos

Vietnam

Cambodia

Indonesia

Brunei

Myanmar

SOUTHEAST ASIA

One of the great things about St. Louis's diversity is its ethnic associations. The Filipino-American Association of Missouri includes in its mission to "share our culture with our adoptive and extended family in the United States." These active Filipino Americans simultaneously preserve their heritage while expanding the horizons of everyday St. Louisans through their scholarship program, English classes, literacy projects, cooking classes, and various community service ventures. The contributions of these valuable men and women to their new city belie the original, difficult relationship between the Philippines and the United States.

During the imperialistic years at the turn of the twentieth century, the small Philippine nation became a territory of the United States after America helped drive out the Spanish. It was a cruel occupation, and the Filipinos felt defeated and rightly resentful. To dilute the negative public opinion, the 1904 World's Fair in St. Louis was the backdrop for a propaganda extravaganza. The "native" displays featured aboriginals from countries around the world, and the Philippines was the largest and grandest. The exhibition achieved the goal of representing the Filipinos as savage and uncivilized. St. Louis lore still contends that the Dogtown neighborhood south of Forest Park was so named for the dogs butchered

there and eaten by the Filipino Igorot tribe while at the fair. Additionally, the Wydown Middle School in Clayton, which sits on the site of the Igorot Village, once fielded an Igorrote football team. Many walked away from the World's Fair with the notion that the United States was right to conquer the island nation—that was the only way to make those poor people civilized. After bouts of self-government and a stint of Japanese rule, the Philippines finally became an independent nation in 1946.

After a change in the immigration law in 1965, the door to the United States opened for citizens of Southeast Asia, whose countries include Brunei, Myanmar, Cambodia, East Timor, Indonesia, Laos, Malaysia, the Philippines, Singapore, Thailand, and Vietnam. Many of these Southeast Asians, fleeing political unrest, found their way to St. Louis in the mid-1970s and later. This includes the Vietnamese, now the city's second-largest immigrant group after the Bosnians. To conquer the language barrier, the St. Louis Public Schools' extensive English as a Second

Language/Bilingual/Migrant Program began in 1980 with a few Vietnamese students at Roosevelt High School.

Southeast Asians represent a variety of religions, including Buddhism, Christianity, Islam, Hinduism, and others. Temples and churches of all religious affiliations serve this population of St. Louisans, including the Vien Minh Temple on Bulwer Avenue, Wat Buddhamanee Rattanaram Temple on Cherokee, Vo Luong Quang Vietnam Temple on Heege Road, Resurrection of Our Lord Catholic Parish on Meramec, Wat Phrasriratanaram Buddhist Temple in Florissant, and Emmanuel Vietnamese Baptist Church on Magnolia Avenue. Restaurants, grocery stores, and bakeries offering Thai, Vietnamese, Laotian, and other Southeast Asian cuisine dot the region, especially along South Grand between Arsenal and Gravois. Every St. Louisan should sample food from Guerrilla Street Food, a truck with delicious Filipino cuisine.

Collectively, Asian Americans have a dynamic presence in St. Louis, boasting large memberships in such groups as the Young Asian-American Professional Association, the Asian-American

Chamber of Commerce, and the St. Louis Chapter of Asian Pacific American Advocates. Nation-specific groups such as the Filipino Student Association of Saint Louis University add youth and educational and cultural value to the diverse ethnic tapestry of St. Louis.

MIDDLE EAST AND NORTH AFRICA

MIDDLE EAST AND NORTH AFRICA

Afghani

Some Afghani immigrants came to St. Louis as early as the 1960s, largely for employment opportunities. Like today's immigrants from Afghanistan, those early newcomers represented a diverse nation made up of many cultures, ethnic groups, and religions, including the most populous religion, Islam. The Islamic Foundation of Greater St. Louis, a nonprofit entity, was established in 1974. Today, the foundation holds prayers in two St. Louis mosques, Masjid Bilal and Daar-ul-Islam Masjid, as well as educational programs, social activities, and weekend classes for kids. Masjid Bilal is the oldest in St. Louis, and is located on the campus of Saint Louis University. While Islamic centers, mosques, and *masjids* are located all around St. Louis, the largest Islamic center is located on Weidman Road in Ballwin, a picturesque St. Louis suburb.

Like other predominately Islamic nations, Afghanistan's varying cultures influence their interpretations of the Quran, making the religion as diverse as its people. When Afghanis immigrate to St. Louis, they bring these differences with them. They pray in St. Louis's masjids alongside local Muslims and others from around the world.

St. Louis has provided refuge for many Afghanis. Additionally, the city offers Afghani women opportunities that are not available to them in their home country. One Afghani refugee worked as an interpreter for St. Louis's International Institute, serving many new refugees. The *St. Louis Beacon* described her service as "delicate work, respecting one culture while explaining another." And so the Afghanis begin their new journey, enriching their lives as well as those of their new fellow St. Louisans.

Egyptian

Egyptians have been immigrating to St. Louis since the late 1960s. Many of the earliest immigrants arrived with degrees in higher education and have played a significant role in the science, technology, and medical communities. Today, there are a significant number of Egyptian Americans who live in Olivette and Creve Coeur. Those of Egyptian descent represent many faiths, and the St. Mary & St. Abraam Coptic Orthodox Church on Ross Avenue serves as one of the community centers. The Coptic-style church building was completed in 1994, though the church was originally founded in 1976. The church offers services in English as well as Coptic and Arabic languages, in keeping with traditional Coptic and Egyptian traditions.

Iranian

Iranians from all walks of life have immigrated to St. Louis in waves. The earliest group arrived in the mid- to late 1960s as professionals, predominately physicians, who joined St. Louis's premier medical community. A larger wave of Iranians immigrated to St. Louis in the 1980s and 1990s, many seeking higher education. Iranian immigrants of the Bahá'i faith came to St. Louis as refugees in the early twenty-first century, fleeing religious persecution. Most recently, well-educated young Iranians have arrived to continue their studies in St. Louis universities.

Generations of Iranian Americans have made St. Louis their home. Members of this community founded the Iranian American Cultural Society of the Midwest "to promote cultural and social contacts among the Iranian community, among Iranians and Americans, and anyone interested in Iranian culture." The Iranian-American Cultural Association of Missouri has a wider agenda, "to promote human rights and tolerance."

While the majority of Iranian immigrants practice Islam, the Iranian American community represents a multitude of religions. Among the mosques in St. Louis, the Shiite mosque in Wildwood, Dar-al-Zahra, is home to many immigrants from Iran. Many Christians attend the Iranian Church of St. Louis, located in Chesterfield on North Outer Forty Road.

Regardless of your heritage, go to Café Natasha in the University City Loop for delicious Persian fare. Or, head over to Kabob International on South Grand, where Persia meets St. Louis. Move over, toasted ravioli!

Iraqi

The United States closed its doors to Iraqi refugees after the September 11, 2001, attacks. In 2005, Iraqi citizens were again allowed into the resettlement program, and for nearly a decade afterward refugees from the war-torn country have made their way into the United States. In St. Louis, men, women, and children from Iraq have made up one of the largest resettlement groups in recent years. With the help of the International Institute and service organizations, Iraqi refugees readily adapt to their new surroundings in St. Louis.

St. Louisans have done more than just welcome Iraqis into the Gateway City. The Iraqi Student Project is described as "a grass-roots effort to help war-displaced Iraqi students acquire an undergraduate education." The program now enrolls sixty-two Iraqi students at forty-eight American universities, including St. Louis's Fontbonne University.

Recognizing that women in Iraq lack individual protections taken for granted in the United States, the Women Lawyers' Association of Greater St. Louis found a way to offer support. The group speaks via video conference with female attorneys in Iraq, advising on navigating a legal system unfriendly to women. The Iraqi attorneys risk serious retribution for their participation. The bridge between the women of St. Louis and those in Iraq is constructed of professional camaraderie and friendship.

And yet the relationship between the United States and Iraq is complex. Regardless of any political leanings, St. Louis was the first city to throw a parade for men and women of the military who served in Iraq. The parade drew huge crowds of cheering people from St. Louis and beyond.

Although Islam is by far the most widely practiced religion in Iraq, faith is as varied as its geographic regions and ethnic populations. The people bring this diversity with them as they immigrate. Iraqis have adapted, finding spiritual homes in St. Louis in the many mosques that dot the region.

Stop into the Baghdad Market on Grand for some exotic food, and remember that it takes moxie to start from scratch in a new city so different from home, all in the name of finding a better life. The Iraqi refugees have done just that, whether they arrived decades ago or months ago. If it is moxie they bring, then St. Louis is the perfect place for them.

Pakistani

In 1968, a change in immigration law opened the door to new immigrants from around the world. That year, the Nationality and Immigration Act voided the national origins component. Under that part of the law, certain nations, specifically those in Europe and China, had quotas for immigration based on existing representation in the United States. With that change, immigrants from around the globe, especially those from predominantly Muslim nations, found their way to St. Louis. In this wave, Pakistanis, many highly educated, made St. Louis their home. Ever since, countrymen and relatives have joined the early arrivals.

The Salam Free Clinic was established in 2008 by a group of Muslim doctors, many of them Pakistani. Embodying the spirit of working together for the greater good, the clinic was set in a Christian church in north St. Louis, where the doctors offered care to those who could not afford a traditional visit to the doctor. The trend continued, as reported by the *St. Louis Post-Dispatch*: "In September 2011, the Association of Physicians of Pakistani Descent of North America established a clinic providing free dental, ophthalmologic, pediatric, and pain-management services on Sundays at the Balal Mosque

on Saint Louis University's campus." Also in 2011, the Islamic Foundation of Greater St. Louis, in partnership with Volunteers in Medicine, opened a similar clinic on Manchester Road in Manchester, a St. Louis suburb.

Pakistani Muslims living in St. Louis are among Muslims from more than two dozen nations. While most agree that the basic tenets of Islam are the same, all bring with them ethnic and cultural differences that can make the practice of Islam as diverse as their homelands. Such variation adds to the mosaic that is St. Louis.

For a taste of Pakistan, St. Louisans are fortunate to have many options for South Asian and Middle Eastern cuisine. Two of the finest are located in St. Louis County. Seema Enterprises is a grocery store on Page Avenue in Olivette. The Mideast Market, a store and dine-in establishment on Manchester Road in Ballwin, will challenge your skills in the kitchen and gratify your taste buds.

Turkish

Turkey is one of those nations whose people grew out of centuries of change: fluctuating boundaries, ever-changing ruling dynasties, and shifting population groups. As a result, early Turkish immigrants who arrived in St. Louis were documented as anything from Slavic to Armenian. Today, St. Louis Turks continue their melting-pot traditions by working to strengthen St. Louis's intercultural community. This philosophy of cohesion is one of the basic tenets of the Turkish-American Society of Missouri. The group seeks to "enrich the experience of the entire community" through diversity, inclusion, and respect for all. St. Louisans can ponder the group's noble contributions while dining at Aya Sofia on Chippewa, which serves some of the finest Turkish cuisine in all the Midwest.

EUROPE

EUROPE

Bosnian and Herzegovinian

Bosnians are now one of the largest ethnic communities in St. Louis. Estimated at fifty thousand, the local community is the largest concentration of Bosnians outside of Bosnia-Herzegovina. In fact, parts of south St. Louis around the famous Bevo Mill are now called "Little Bosnia."

Once part of Yugoslavia, Bosnia-Herzegovina was at the center of the violent dissolution between 1991 and 1995 of the once-Communist state in south central Europe, which resulted in separate countries for the six principal Yugoslav republics: Bosnia-Herzegovina, Croatia, Macedonia, Montenegro, Serbia, and Slovenia.

The Bosnians who came to St. Louis beginning in the mid-1990s were escaping the worst violence in Europe since the end of World War II, which included a systematic campaign of genocidal attacks under the euphemism of ethnic cleansing. As a result, more than one hundred thousand Bosnians lost their lives and two million people were displaced out of a total population of just over four million.

The first war refugees to arrive in St. Louis were survivors of a network of concentration camps in northwest Bosnia where large numbers of Bosnian Muslims and Catholics had been subjected to mass killing, torture, and systematic rape at the hands of ultranationalist Serbs as part of a campaign of terror and territorial control.

Many of the first arrivals here came from the Bosnian city of Prijedor, from which fifty thousand Muslim and Catholic Croat citizens had been violently expelled. They were met by fellow Bosnians who had come to St. Louis before the 1992 war and had been enlisted as volunteers by the International Institute to help with initial resettlement efforts.

The International Institute was asked by the U.S. State Department to assess the city's capacity to receive Bosnian refugees who had no family ties in the United States. St. Louis was chosen as a major resettlement site because of the low cost of living, good housing stock in the city, and availability of light manufacturing jobs.

The International Institute also located, identified, and organized a cohort of local Bosnians who could welcome the newly arriving refugees in their own language and assist them in resettling in St. Louis. Ermina and Suljo Grbic, who later opened the popular Grbic Restaurant, welcomed many new refugees into their home and led efforts to assist new arrivals.

The Bosnians quickly established themselves as a positive presence in St. Louis, settling mostly in South City and bringing with them tight extended families, a strong work ethic, and resourceful skills in home repair that made them well liked by landlords who quickly noticed that their apartments were often in better shape after their Bosnian tenants moved in.

The city government took notice of the stabilizing effect the Bosnian community was having in once-deteriorating sections of the city and reached out to the Bosnian community to provide assistance.

Once settled, Bosnians began to open neighborhood businesses that catered to their own community, including small grocery stores, bakeries, coffee shops, and travel agencies. In 1994, a Bosnian cultural club was opened in a donated warehouse space whose ground floor served as a free thrift shop filled with second-hand furniture, clothing, and household items for new refugees.

Like the former Yugoslavia, Bosnia-Herzegovina was a multiethnic society comprising Muslims, Orthodox Christian Serbs, Roman Catholic Croats, Jews, Roma, Ukrainians, and others before the war. As the principal victims of the war, the majority of Bosnian refugees who came to St. Louis were Muslim, with smaller numbers of Catholics and those of mixed religious heritage.

To provide for the spiritual needs of local Bosnians, Imam Muhamed Hasic was invited to come to St. Louis to establish an organized religious community and mosque. A tall, slim minaret is now part of the skyline near Kingshighway and Chippewa at a former bank building that became the first Bosnian mosque in St. Louis. Two other mosques have followed in St. Louis County, reflecting the gradual migration of the Bosnian community into South County.

As word spread of the success and warm welcome for the St. Louis Bosnian community, Bosnian refugees from other parts of the country became a secondary migration that added to the size and strength of the local population. Twenty years after their initial resettlement, Bosnians in St. Louis have achieved remarkable success in business, media, education, and the arts. In July 2014, as a gift to the city of St. Louis, the Bosnian community donated a monument in the center of the Bevo neighborhood—a "Sebilj" modeled on one that sits in the center of the Bosnian capital of Sarajevo.

Despite their numerous accomplishments, Bosnians have not forgotten the circumstances that brought them here. Each year, on July 11, hundreds of Bosnians gather to commemorate the 1995 genocide in the town of Srebrenica, during which more than

eight thousand Bosnian men and boys were killed. Large numbers of Srebrenica survivors later came to St. Louis. While tragedy and sorrow created the Bosnian community here, new beginnings and opportunities are building a brighter future for the Bosnians and for all those who now call them neighbors and friends.

CENTRAL AMERICA AND THE CARIBBEAN

CENTRAL AMERICA AND THE CARIBBEAN

Belizean

St. Louis immigrants from Belize are largely represented by the Belize Association of St. Louis. The organization, founded in 1997, comprises Belizean immigrants as well as those interested in the nation of Belize. Celebrating Belizean culture, the association serves as both a social and philanthropic organization, aiding Belizeans in Belize as well as St. Louis.

Haitian

Haitians immigrated to St. Louis predominately in two waves. The first arrived in the 1950s as medical residents at Homer G. Phillips Hospital, one of the few hospitals in the United States open to black medical professionals for training. The next wave of Haitian immigrants sought refuge in St. Louis in the early 1990s, escaping military oppression.

While St. Louisans have welcomed and benefited from the contributions of the Haitian settlers, they also extend their interest to the Haitian homeland. Multiple organizations exist with the mission of assisting those who remain in Haiti. Meds for Food and Kids, Haitians Helping Haitians, and the Haitian Orphan Project are among the St. Louis organizations working to better the lives of current residents of Haiti.

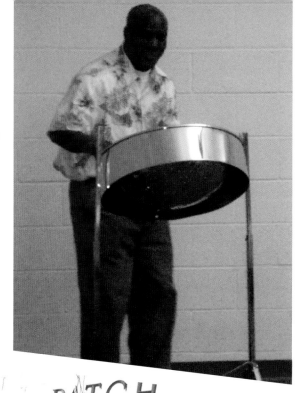

Caribbean

Immigrants from the many countries of the Caribbean are represented by the Caribbean Association of St. Louis. Regardless of nationality, membership is open to all residents of greater St. Louis. The group's mission is "to create an awareness of and promote an appreciation for the culture and heritage of the Caribbean." In addition to its social activities, the organization works philanthropically for the people of the Caribbean and St. Louis, including a scholarship program for graduating high school and college students of Caribbean descent.

SOUTH AMERICA

Brazilian

Colombian

Guyanese

SOUTH AMERICA

Brazilian

Brazilian immigration to St. Louis took place largely in the late 1980s through the 1990s. Faced with economic instability in Brazil, many sought better employment and educational opportunities in the Gateway City. While Washington University and the University of Missouri–St. Louis enticed students, major St. Louis corporations such as Monsanto, Nestlé Purina, and Bunge North America, with global markets and Brazilian connections, beckoned Brazilian scientists, engineers, and other industry leaders. Additionally, Brown Shoe and Anheuser-Busch InBev, St. Louis powerhouses with Brazilian connections, attracted Brazilian immigrants looking for better economic possibilities in St. Louis.

Of those Brazilian immigrants who arrived in the 1990s, many found camaraderie at Brandt's Café in the Loop. Then and now, they satisfy their tastes for home at Jays International Food Company on South Grand. While they live throughout the metropolitan area without a specific enclave, Brazilians in St. Louis provide a variety of ethnic restaurants and markets.

Viva Brasil is a nonprofit association founded in St. Louis in 2011. Begun by a group of immigrant Brazilian mothers, its mission is to promote the

Brazilian culture in the St. Louis region, and to maintain the Brazilian cultural heritage. The association now offers Portuguese classes. While Brazilians' religious preferences vary, some families sponsor a Catholic Mass in Portuguese. Brazilian immigrants brought revelry with them to St. Louis, including the festivities of Mardi Gras (Carnival) and June summer festivals. *Viva Brasil*!

Colombian

Citizens from Colombia have lived in St. Louis since the early 1940s. Taking advantage of St. Louis's academic institutions, employment opportunities, and welcoming character, Colombian Americans learned English, raised families, and contributed to the diversity of St. Louis. Like those who arrived generations before them, the story remains the same for recent Colombian immigrants. These numbers include political refugees who sought refuge in St. Louis in the early twenty-first century. Though the long-standing Colombian Society has disbanded, Colombian Americans in St. Louis continue to gather socially, often in conjunction with other Hispanic groups in the region.

Guyanese

In 1990, Georgetown, Guyana, joined St. Louis in the Sister Cities program. St. Louisans have benefited from this relationship, in which the goals are to "encourage friendship and economic cooperation," as well as exchange ideas and information. In addition to other research ventures between Guyanese and St. Louis institutions, the University of Missouri–St. Louis has offered a study abroad program featuring biodiversity on one of Guyana's many rivers. The relationship with St. Louis's Guyanese immigrants goes beyond welcoming the newcomers. It is one that includes science, economics, and friendship.

AFRICA

AFRICA

Burundian

Ethnic and political conflicts caused violence in Burundi in 1972. That year, many Burundian survivors of the unrest fled to the nearby African countries of Rwanda, Tanzania, and what is now the Democratic Republic of Congo. Civil unrest continued in Burundi through the 1990s. Many Burundians were further displaced during the Rwandan genocide in 1994.

After many difficult years as refugees, the United States has been resettling ethnic Burundians since 2006. St. Louis is not one of the American cities that received the majority of the refugees, but a small number of Burundians have found a home here. Through the International Institute's resettlement program, new immigrants from Burundi have a fresh start—economically, educationally, and socially.

The New City Fellowship in South City offers multiple educational programs and services to immigrants of all ethnicities. On their own, Burundians contribute fortitude and inner strength to the character of St. Louis. Both the city and the Burundian immigrants celebrate their arrival.

Congolese

Congolese immigrants first arrived in St. Louis in the 1980s. Many of these immigrants were well educated and seeking employment. Most from the Democratic Republic of Congo came around the year 2000 as refugees, fleeing ethnic violence. Some made their way to St. Louis after living in refugee camps in other countries before being granted passage to the United States. With help from the International Institute and the former African Mutual Assistance Association of Missouri, Congolese refugees have found a home in St. Louis. The refugees represent the faiths of Islam, Christianity, and others, yet faith-based organizations and churches of all faiths offer assistance to the new arrivals.

Eritrean

Immigrants from Eritrea first arrived in St. Louis in the 1970s. There were only a few of them, primarily seeking a higher education. Then, in the early 1980s, the demographic of Eritrean immigrants changed. An influx of refugees fled the hardships of the war for independence of Eritrea. The Eritrean community of St. Louis banded together, and today is represented by over three hundred households.

Eritrean community leaders established the Red Sea Eritrean Community Center with the mission "to promote cultural vibrancy of the Eritrean heritage by strengthening family life, uplifting each other, educating our children, and cultivating the diverse historical traditions among Eritreans as well as area residents for mutual understanding." The group first rented space at the International Institute, then at Mt. Olive Church. In 2010, the group purchased its building on North Grand, and there the Red Sea Eritrean Community Center is a vibrant beacon for the St. Louis Eritrean community. Their philosophy says it all: "We believe with the understanding of our country's culture, we can better influence the ethnic diversity of the St. Louis region."

Ethiopian

Ethiopian immigrants arrived seeking political asylum and a new beginning in the late 1980s. Many of those were university educated in Ethiopia. But in the late 1990s, Ethiopians came to St. Louis by way of a refugee program. Aided by organizations such as the International Institute and the former African Mutual Assistance

Association of Missouri, these Ethiopians began to integrate themselves into the fabric of the city.

The Habesha people from the northern part of Ethiopia have formed a community based on their common ethnic background. The St. Louis Habesha Network works to "build a networking community that brings together the Habesha people of St. Louis and its surrounding areas through an exchange of ideas and the sharing of information, interests, and resources." The group's core values dictate that they are nonpolitical, nonreligious, and positive—perfect for the diverse nature of St. Louis. Enjoy the sounds of the Habesha community by listening to STL Habesha Radio.

Ethiopians worship in many faiths. Some have found a spiritual home at one of three churches: Debre Nazreth St. Mary and St. Gabriel Ethiopian Orthodox Tewahedo Church in the Vinita Park neighborhood, the Redeemer of the World Evangelical Church in Overland, and New City Fellowship in South City.

Ghanaian

Ghanaians first arrived in St. Louis in the 1960s, after their country's independence. Most of those

early arrivals were well educated, and they sought further education and employment in St. Louis. By the 1990s, Ghanaian Americans in St. Louis gathered socially, bonded by their culture. The nonprofit Ghanaian Association of St. Louis was formed in 2011. The group states, "Our primary goal is to build strong bonds and relationships within the Ghanaian community, and give an opportunity for networking through social events."

In addition to welcoming Ghanaian immigrants, St. Louisans have worked to strengthen ties with Ghana. In 2013, Washington University chancellor Mark S. Wrighton traveled to Ghana. There, he and officials from the University of Ghana formally signed a partnership agreement that promoted collaborative research and education between the two institutions. This was achieved through Washington University's McDonnell International Scholars Academy, making Ghana the 28th partner and the first from Africa.

In 2014, Ghanaian native and Maryville University graduate Mawuyrami Akoto returned to Ghana. There, she worked in her field of music therapy with special needs students and founded the nonprofit Music Therapy Association of Ghana. Her outreach bridges her life in St. Louis with her home country, providing innovative services to children.

Liberian

Most members of St. Louis's Liberian community arrived as refugees around the turn of this century. Today, ethnic Liberians celebrate their common heritage through the Liberian Association of Missouri. Founded in 2003, the group assists newly arrived Liberian refugees in adapting to their new St. Louis home, while promoting Liberian culture through local events. The association launched its Together against Ebola campaign in 2014. Through this initiative, St. Louis Liberians joined fellow St. Louisans in raising money and awareness for Liberians who suffer in Africa.

Senegalese

Senegalese immigrants first arrived in St. Louis in the 1980s, seeking opportunity and education. Most Senegalese students encountered little difficulty in assimilating, as many spoke English. Others utilized their skills to open small businesses in trades involving hair braiding, clothing, and restaurants. Today, immigrants from Senegal can be found in academia, medicine, and all levels of business.

In 1996, the cities of St. Louis, Missouri, and Saint-Louis, Senegal, formed a sister city relationship. Through the years, this union has presented opportunities that have benefited St. Louisans of both countries in numerous ways. These include educational and cultural exchanges through the Fulbright Program, St. Louis Public Schools, Webster University, Saint Louis University, Saint Louis Science Center, Saint Louis Art Museum, St. Louis Community College, Washington University, and the Missouri alumni of the Education Policy Fellowship Program.

With the sister city organization, the communities have established the eye glasses program Pair Up for the residents in Saint-Louis, Senegal, as well as a sanitation program funded by the Bill and Melinda Gates Foundation.

The Senegalese Association was founded in St. Louis in 2010. The association works to "defend and promote Senegalese culture and values" in St. Louis, "provide a venue for fellowship with other Senegalese living in the St. Louis area, regardless of their religious, political, or philosophical beliefs and ideas," and "assist each other in challenging times." In so doing, the association conducts a variety of social events for its members. The Senegalese Association also assists with Washington University's annual African Film Festival. The final mission of the Senegalese Association represents the Senegalese community in St. Louis: "take an active part in the economic development of the Senegalese community in America as well as in Senegal." The cities of St. Louis and Saint-Louis are better for it.

Somalian

The decades of unrest in Somalia prompted much of the migration of Somalians to the United States. Somalians comprise the third-largest refugee group in St. Louis. Many have formed a cohesive community in St. Louis, while others live in the St. Louis suburbs. Together and independently, they are learning English, finding employment, and attending churches and mosques. Welcomed by their new city, the Somalians are transforming St. Louis from asylum to home.

South African

One South African immigrant noted that some South African natives in St. Louis "get together to reminisce, speak our language, use our slang, and eat our traditional food." Others connect on social media, bonded by their common heritage. Recent arrivals are welcomed by those who have lived in St. Louis for as long as twenty-five years. South African–Americans live all around the St. Louis region and work in a variety of professions, helping make St. Louis a great and diverse city.

HISPANIC COMMUNITIES

HISPANIC COMMUNITIES

"*Hispanic culture* is kind of like saying *white culture*. Mexicans are so different from Argentinians, despite their common language, that it's more like Americans and New Zealanders being put in the same cultural group." These are the insights of Father Anthony Ochoa of St. Cecilia Catholic Church on Louisiana Avenue in south St. Louis. St. Cecilia Parish is nearly as old as St. Louis, but its purpose changed in 2005 when the archbishop named it the "personal parish for the faithful of Hispanic language and heritage." The church holds a full house during its services, most of which are held in Spanish.

It's helpful to remember that "Hispanic" means "Spanish speaking," while "Latino" refers to people of Latin American heritage. As noted by Father Anthony Ochoa, the word "Hispanic" tends to generalize anyone who hails from any country south of the United States. It is impressive that immigrants from south of the border use their commonalities as Hispanics to help them assimilate into the fabric of St. Louis, all while maintaining the identity of their home countries.

Trendy and artsy Cherokee Street, particularly west of Jefferson Avenue, bustles with Hispanic culture. The shops, markets, and restaurants serve the Hispanic and multicultural neighborhoods surrounding this enclave. Latinos, specifically immigrants from Mexico, began settling in this community in the early 1980s. In celebration of Hispanic culture in another part of the St. Louis area, St. Louisans pour into north St. Louis County, an area with a growing Hispanic community, for their annual Fiesta in Florissant for music, dancing, art, and fabulous food. Even larger is the Greater St. Louis Hispanic Festival at Soulard Park near 7th Street and Lafayette, next to Soulard Market. There, St. Louisans of all walks of life join in celebrating the common heritage of those from Hispanic nations.

The Hispanic Arts Council of St. Louis was created in 1996, with the mission "to promote the excellence of the Hispanic culture through arts and educational events." Among other events and activities, the group hosts concerts of high-profile Latino musicians at the Sheldon Concert Hall. The organization raises funds for college scholarships for first-generation Latino youth. The Hispanic Chamber of Commerce of Metropolitan St. Louis was established in 1982, and has worked to support and promote Hispanic small businesses. Comprising Hispanic and non-Hispanic organizations and professionals, the chamber promotes business development for a "better and stronger St. Louis region."

The majority of Hispanics living in St. Louis came to the Gateway City in recent years. Many of these hearty immigrants contribute greatly to St. Louis's economic heartbeat through roll-up-your-sleeves manual labor. St. Louis extended its hand to some of the recent influx of children from Central America who, fleeing unspeakable hardship, found their way into the United States. St. Louis has provided them with a safe place to lay their heads while they await their futures.

Casa de Salud, a health-care clinic located on the medical campus of Saint Louis University, was established to provide high-quality medical services for uninsured and underinsured patients. The clinic focuses on newly arrived immigrants and refugees. Other St. Louis universities offer care and opportunities, such as the Center for Latino Family Research, founded in 2006 at the Brown School at Washington University, and the Latino Youth Tutoring/ Mentoring Programs, also at Washington University. Students at the University of Missouri–St. Louis organized the Hispanic Latino Association, and the University of Missouri presents the annual Cambio de Colores Conference, a venue to discuss means for the successful transition of new immigrants into Missouri communities.

Some Latino immigrants came as early as the 1940s. Most were professionals, like those from Argentina. Many Venezuelan professionals immigrated in the 1980s. Later, large companies like Monsanto and Purina employed new immigrants from South

American countries. Argentinians enjoy a relationship with Anheuser-Busch InBev, as the brewing powerhouse runs a global center in that South American nation. As the Latinos settled in St. Louis, those with numbers and enthusiasm founded cultural associations, like those from Argentina, Belize, Colombia, Mexico, Peru, Puerto Rico, and Venezuela. Such groups celebrate the immigrants' heritage while contributing to the cultural landscape of their new city.

"The greatest gift the Hispanics can give to the city is its sense of humanity and wonder." Father Anthony Ochoa speaks reverently about the community he serves from the altar at St. Cecilia. Other churches offering services in Spanish include Holy Trinity Catholic Parish in St. Ann and Our Lady of Guadalupe Parish, located on South Florissant Road. The Archdiocese of St. Louis has an Office of Hispanic Ministry to serve St. Louis's Hispanic population.

The list of contributions of the Latinos to the St. Louis community is endless. But let's name a few: all-time great catcher Yadier Molina from Puerto Rico; Fritanga Restaurant on Jefferson Avenue, boasting Nicaraguan food; and FutbolSTL, an incredibly impressive Hispanic soccer league.

That's diverse St. Louis.

ENDNOTES

[1] Missouri History Museum, http://www.mohistory.org/Fair/WF HTML/About/

[2] "Census Shows City Is 'Hollowing Out,'" *St. Louis Post-Dispatch*, February 25, 2011.

[3] "Census Shows City Is 'Hollowing Out,'" *St. Louis Post-Dispatch*, February 25, 2011.

[4] Strauss, J. (2012). "The Economic Impact of Immigration on St. Louis." Saint Louis University: St. Louis.

REFERENCES

American Sokol Centennial, 1865–1965. Chicago: Berwyn Press, 1965.

Baumann, Timothy E. "Evidence Unearthed: Digging into Scott Joplin's St. Louis." *Gateway*, 29 (2009): 39–49.

"Brief History of the Polish Community." Ethnic Heritage, Local History File, St. Louis County Library History and Genealogy Department.

Brunsmann, Sandra M. *Early Irish Settlers in St. Louis, Missouri and Dogtown Neighborhood*. St. Louis: S. M. Brunsmann, 2000.

Cassens, David E. "The Bulgarian Colony of Southwestern Illinois, 1900–1920." *Illinois Historical Journal*, 84 (Spring 1991): 15–24.

Cassens, David E. "Helpless Wanderers in a Strange Land: The Rev. Tzvetko Bagranoff and the Bulgarian Community in Southwestern Illinois." *Gateway Heritage*, 14, no. 2 (Fall 1993): 54–65.

Choi, Kyung Soo. "The Assimilation of Korean Immigrants in the St. Louis Area." Dissertation, St. Louis University, 1982.

Christian, Shirley. *Before Lewis and Clark: The Story of the Chouteaus, the French Dynasty That Ruled America's Frontier*. New York: Farrar, Straus and Giroux, 2004.

City Plan Commission. Map of the city of St. Louis showing population distribution, 1930–1935. Missouri History Museum Library and Research Center.

Corbett, Katharine T., and Mary E. Seematter. "No Crystal Stair: Black St. Louis, 1920–1940." *Gateway Heritage*, 16, no. 2 (Fall 1995): 82–88.

Corzine, Jay, and Irene Dabrowski. "The Ethnic Factor and Neighborhood Stability: The Czechs in Soulard and South St. Louis." *Bulletin of the Missouri Historical Society* (January 1977): 87–93.

Davies, Phillips G., trans. "Reverend R. D. Thomas's 'Welsh in Missouri, 1872.'" *Missouri Historical Review*, 72, no. 2 (January 1978): 154–161.

DeChenne, David. "Hungry Hollow: Bulgarian Immigrant Life in Granite City, Illinois, 1904–1921." *Gateway Heritage*, 11, no. 1 (Summer 1990): 52-61.

Diamond, Etan. "Kerry Patch: Irish Immigrant Life in St. Louis." *Gateway Heritage*, 10, no. 2 (Fall 1989): 22–31.

Dickey, Michael. *The People of the River's Mouth: In Search of the Missouria Indians.* Columbia: University of Missouri Press, 2011.

Dolan, Ellen Meara. *The Saint Louis Irish*. St. Louis: Old St. Patrick's, 1967.

Duden, Gottfried. *Report on a Journey to the Western States of North America and a Stay of Several Years Along the Missouri (During the Years 1824, '25, '26, and 1827).* Edited and translated by James W. Goodrich, George H. Kellner, Elsa Nagel, Adolf E. Schroeder, W. M. Senner. Columbia: State Historical Society of Missouri and the University of Missouri Press, 1980.

Faherty, William Barnaby. *The Saint Louis Portrait.* Tulsa: The Continental Heritage, Inc., 1978.

Faherty, William Barnaby. "St. Louis Mosaic: Community's Heritage Is Enriched by Cultures from Many Lands." Ca. 1982.

Faherty, William Barnaby. *The St. Louis Irish: An Unmatched Celtic Community.* St. Louis: Missouri Historical Society Press, 2001.

Faherty, William Barnaby. *Catholic St. Louis: A Pictorial History*. St. Louis: Reedy Press, 2009.

Fausz, J. Frederick. "Founding St. Louis: A New French Frontier at the End of an Empire." *Gateway*, 29 (2009): 9–23.

Fausz, J. Frederick. *Founding St. Louis: First City of the New West.* Charleston: The History Press, 2011.

Fermin, Jose D. *1904 World's Fair: The Filipino Experience*. Infinity Publishing.com, 2004.

Fox, Tim, ed. *Where We Live: A Guide to St. Louis Communities.* St. Louis: Missouri Historical Society Press, 1995.

Fox, Timothy J. "Where the Czechs Are Is My Home: Lessons from St. Louis's Other Hill." *Gateway Heritage*, 23, no. 4 (Spring 2003): 47–55.

Friesen, Gerhard K., and Walter Schatzberg, eds. *The German Contribution to the Building of the Americas*. Hanover, NH: Clark University Press, 1977.

Gitlin, Jay. "Avec Bien du Regret: The Americanization of Creole St. Louis." *Gateway Heritage*, 9, no. 4 (Spring 1989): 2–11.

Hannon, Robert E., ed., and Jack Zehrt. *St. Louis: Its Neighborhoods and Neighbors, Landmarks and Milestones*. St. Louis: Regional Commerce and Growth Association, 1986.

Harl, Joseph L. *Data Recovery Investigations at the Cochran Gardens Hope VI Housing Development Tract, St. Louis City, Missouri.* St. Louis, Mo.: Archaeological Research Center of St. Louis, 2006.

"Highlights of the Address by Mr. Alex G. Nelson at the 75th Anniversary of the Swedish National Society on November 14th, 1964." Swedish National Historical Society, Missouri History Museum.

Hodes, Frederick A. *Beyond the Frontier: A History of St. Louis to 1821*. Tucson: Patrice Press, 2004.

Hodes, Frederick A. *Rising on the River: St. Louis 1822 to 1850, Explosive Growth from Town to City*. Tooele, Utah: Patrice Press, 2009.

Hoig, Stan. *The Chouteaus: First Family of the Fur Trade*. Albuquerque: University of New Mexico Press, 2008.

Hughes, Christine Human. *Guide to St. Louis Catholic Archdiocesan Parish Records*. St. Louis: St. Louis County Library Special Collections, 2001.

Jack, Bryan M. *The St. Louis African American Community and the Exodusters.* Columbia: University of Missouri Press, 2007.

Jewish historical information. From the collections of the St. Louis Jewish
    Community Archives.

Jolly, Kenneth. "Reaction to Liberation: Official Response to the Black
    Liberation Struggle in St. Louis, Missouri." *Gateway Heritage*, 23, no. 4
    (Spring 2003): 30–39.

Jones, Patricia L. "Whatever Happened to Bohemian Hill?" *Gateway Heritage*, 5,
    no. 3 (Winter 1984–1985): 22–31.

Kargau, Ernst D. *Mercantile, Industrial and Professional Saint Louis*. St. Louis:
    Nixon-Jones Printing Company, 1902.

Ling, Huping. *Chinese in St. Louis: From Enclave to Cultural Community*.
    Philadelphia: Temple University Press, 2004.

Ling, Huping. *Chinese in St. Louis, 1857–2007*. Charleston: Arcadia
    Publishing, 2007.

Lovrich, Frank M. "The Dalmatian Yugoslavs in Louisiana." *Louisiana History:
    The Journal of the Louisiana Historical Association*, vol. 8, no. 2
    (Spring 1967): 149.

Marfisi, Eleanore Berra. *The Hill: Its History, Its Recipes*. St. Louis: G. Bradley
    Publishing, Inc., 2003.

Marfisi, Eleanore Berra. *St. Louis Italians: The Hill and Beyond*. St. Louis: G.
    Bradley Publishing, Inc., 2008.

Matsakis, Aphrodite. *Growing Up Greek in St. Louis*. Chicago: Arcadia
    Publishing, 2002.

Mattson, Beulah. *110: Gethsemane Lutheran Church, 1894–2004*. The
    Messenger, 2004.

Merkel, Jim. *Beer, Brats, and Baseball: St. Louis Germans*. St. Louis: Reedy
    Press, 2012.

Montague, William L. *The Saint Louis Business Directory for 1853–4*. St. Louis: E.
    A. Lewis, 1853.

Moore, Benjamin. "Who Was John Gergen? Unraveling the Identity of an Early
    Twentieth-Century Immigrant." *Gateway*, 26, no. 3
    (Spring 2006): 11–23.

Mormino, Gary. "Lombard Roots: From Steerage to the Hill." *Gateway Heritage*, 1,
    no. 3 (Winter 1980): 3–13.

Mormino, Gary. *Immigrants on the Hill: Italian-Americans in St. Louis, 1882–1982*.
    Urbana: University of Illinois Press, 1986.

Nationalities of Greater St. Louis. Compiled by the International Folklore
    Federation of Greater St. Louis, ca. 1982.

Nemec, Slavko. Povijest Hrvatske Naseobine u St. Louisu, Mo., 1862–1931
    [History of Croatian Settlement in St. Louis, Mo., 1862–1931]. San Carlos, CA:
    Ragusan Press, 1931.

Olson, Audrey L. "St. Louis Germans, 1850–1920: The Nature of an Immigrant
    Community and Its Relation to the Assimilation Process." Dissertation,
    Department of History, University of Kansas, 1980.

Person, Sharon. *Standing Up for Indians: Baptism Registers as an Untapped Source for Multicultural Relations in St. Louis, 1766–1821*. Naperville, IL: Center for French Colonial Studies, 2010.

Pickard, Elizabeth A. "Opening the Gates: Segregation, Desegregation, and the Story of Lewis Place." *Gateway*, 26, no. 2 (Fall 2005): 16–27.

Pilapil, Virgilio R. *Touring the Legacy of the 1904 St. Louis World's Fair: With Special Attention to the Philippine Exhibit*. House of Isidoro Press, 2004.

Primm, James Neal. *Lion of the Valley: St. Louis, Missouri, 1764–1980*. St. Louis: Missouri Historical Society Press, 1998.

Rodabough, John. *Frenchtown*. St. Louis: Sunrise Publishing Company, Inc., 1980.

St. Louis Gruetli Verein Records, 1850–1962. Missouri History Museum Archives.

St. Louis Japanese American Citizens League Records, 1906–1988. Collection Guide, State Historical Society of Missouri.

St. Lucas Evangelical Lutheran Church: 100th Anniversary, 1905–2005. St. Louis: St. Lucas Evangelical Church, 2005.

St. Raymond's Maronite Catholic Church. *Lebanon and Its Cuisine*. St. Louis: St. Raymond's Maronite Catholic Church, 1992.

Sandweiss, Lee Ann. *Seeking St. Louis: Voices from a River City, 1670–2000*. St. Louis: Missouri Historical Society Press, 2000.

Senyszyn, M. Angela, Sister, O.S.F. "The Polish-Born Immigrant in Saint Louis, 1860–1900." Thesis, University of Missouri–St. Louis, 1979.

Serbian Eastern Orthodox Church-School Parish. *Holy Trinity of St. Louis, Missouri: 100 Years of History in Celebration of Our Centennial Anniversary, November 2009.* St. Louis: Serbian Eastern Orthodox Church, 2009.

Seventy-Fifth Anniversary Album, 1917–1992: Saint Nicholas Greek Orthodox Church. St. Louis, 1992.

65th Anniversary, 1909–1974, St. Michael the Archangel Russian Orthodox Church. St. Louis: 1975.

Souvenir Book of Holy Trinity Slovak Parish, St. Louis, Missouri. St. Louis: Holy Trinity Slovak Parish, 1973.

Stadler, Frances Hurd. *St. Louis: From Laclede to Land Clearance.* St. Louis: Radio Station KSD and Kriegshauser Mortuaries, 1962.

Stellos, Marie Helen. "The Greek Community in St. Louis (1900–1967): Its Agencies for Value Transmission." Ann Arbor, Michigan: UMI Dissertation Services, 1968.

Swierenga, Robert P. "The Dutch Transplanting in Michigan and the Midwest." Lecture, 111th Annual Meeting of the Historical Society of Michigan, Grand Rapids, Michigan, October 4, 1985.

Tanner, Marcus. *Croatia: A Nation Forged in War.* New Haven: Yale University Press, 1997.

Thorp, Adam. "Remnant of a Vanished City to Ornament New Subway Restaurant." *Prep News* (St. Louis University High School newspaper). September 5, 2013.

Toft, Carolyn Hewes, ed. *Carondelet: The Ethnic Heritage of an Urban Neighborhood.* St. Louis: Washington University, 1975.

Walker, Alicia. *Savage to Civilized: The Imperial Agenda on Display at the St. Louis World's Fair of 1904.* Saarbrücken, Germany: Verlag Dr. Müller, 2008.

Walsh, Joel. "Shining Stars: The Negro Leagues in St. Louis." *Gateway*, 25, no. 3 (Winter 2004–5): 11–21.

Woodhouse, Anne, and Emily Jaycox. "A Mingling of Influences: French, Spanish, and English in Early St. Louis." *Gateway*, 27 (2007): 9–19.

Wright, John. *African Americans in Downtown St. Louis.* Chicago: Arcadia Publishing, 2003.

Wright, John. *Discovering African American St. Louis: A Guide to Historic Sites, Second Edition.* Saint Louis: Missouri Historical Society Press, 2002.

Youngberg, David Jr. "Swedish Council of Saint Louis." *Spotlight* (Autumn 1989).

NEWSPAPER ARTICLES

"Citizenship Is Taught to Illiterate Aliens: Italians, Syrians, Poles, Croatians, Serbians and Russians Enrolled in Classes." *St. Louis Post-Dispatch*, December 14, 1919.

"Czecho-Slovak Mass Meeting Tomorrow." *St. Louis Post-Dispatch*, September 21, 1918.

"Fealty to U.S. of Konta's Magyar Order Challenged." *St. Louis Post-Dispatch*, September 23, 1918.

"Letters from the People: Illogical Women." *St. Louis Post-Dispatch*, November 11, 1909.

"Life in Russia Easier—But I Like It Here." *St. Louis Post-Dispatch*, December 3, 1976.

"Missouri Has 112 Jap Immigrants and 535 Chinese." *St. Louis Post-Dispatch*, May 25, 1913.

"Most Undesirable Immigration." *St. Louis Post-Dispatch*, October 11, 1901.

"The New Immigration Problem." *St. Louis Post-Dispatch*, April 9, 1920.

"Reluctant Americans: Elderly Soviet Jews Make Best of Their New Lives in St. Louis." *Clayton Citizen Journal*, July 31, 1987.

"Rigid Restriction of Immigration Urged by Secretary Hughes." *St. Louis Post-Dispatch*, April 20, 1921.

"St. Louis Democrat Learns That Several Hundred Members of Swiss Colony . . ." *Missouri Republican*, May 30, 1857.

"The Steamer Ben Franklin, from New Orleans, Brought Up 133 Swiss Emigrants . . ." *Missouri Republican*, May 13, 1844.

"Teacher Helps Americanize Soviet Immigrants." *Clayton Citizen Journal*, July 31, 1987.

ACKNOWLEDGMENTS

Grateful thanks are extended to the following individuals and groups who contributed photographs, documents, and stories to the creation of *Ethnic St. Louis*:

Julius "Joe" Adorjan (Honorary Consul, Hungary), Yemi Akande-Bartsch, Inger Andersen (Dutch), Rayo Animashaun, Rev. Daniel Appleyard (South African), Archives of the Archdiocese of St. Louis, Nilantha Bandara, Francisco Benavides (Honorary Consul, Peru), Patricia J. Benson (Honorary Consul, Costa Rica), Michael Bobroff (Honorary Consul, El Salvador), Charles Brown (Mercantile Library), Dallas L. Browne (Honorary Consul, Tanzania), Ruth Bryant (British), Bruce Buckland (Honorary Consul, Japan), David Cassens (Bulgarian and Serbian), Betsy Cohen (Mosaic Project), Cynthia Cosby (African American Heritage Association), Anna Crosslin (International Institute), Fran Debnam (Norwegian Society), Judy Draper (Honorary Consul, Korea), Diane Everman (Jewish Community Archives), Liselotte Fox (Honorary Consul, Sweden), Darlene Green, William Hanna (Egyptian), J. Olu Hassan, Ghazala Hayat (Pakistani), Elizabeth Hayes, Lansing G. Hecker (Honorary Consul, Germany), History and Genealogy Department of the St. Louis County Library Headquarters, Winsome Henry-Ward, John Hoover (Mercantile Library), Carmen Jacob, Marek Jankowicz (Polish), Nanette Lennartz, Anthony Kaminski, Janice Lesane Katambwa, Father Theophn Koja, Kaysong Lee (Korean), Richard Lodge (Honorary Consul, Netherlands), Rev. Paul Macharia (Kenyan), Kathy McGinnis (Institute for Peace and Justice), Joseph B. McGlynn Jr. (Honorary Consul, Ireland), Jasna Meyer, Ph.D. (Croatian), Missouri History Museum Library and Research Center, Jose L. Molina (Honorary Consul, Spain), Bob Moore (National Park Service), Lilian Morath (Swedish), Rev. Leon Mukendi (Congolese), Cecila Nadal, George Nelson (Swedish), Gillian Noero (South African), Dennis Northcott (Missouri History

Museum), Tyler Nguyen, Robert V. Ogrodnik (Honorary Consul, Poland), Javier Orozco (Hispanic Ministry, Archdiocese of St. Louis), Libby Peters (British), Jane Robert (French), Guillermo A. Rodriguez, St. Louis Jewish Community Archives, Rena Schergen, Mercedes de Sebbio, Rabbi Hyim Shafner (South African), Donna Shaheen, Yael Shoroni, Kam S. Sing (Burmese), JoAnna Spanos (Greek), Rev. Stephen Starr (Danish), Melanie Streeper, Connie Taylor, Maria Guadalupa Taxman (Honorary Consul, Honduras), Lisa Tobar, Ibrahim Vajzovic (Bosnian and Herzegovinian), Nasja Wickerhauser, Rachel Wisdom (Norwegian), Aktas Yucel (Turkish).

INDEX